THE PILGRIM'S WAY

Verse

Translations

Prose

Anthology

THE PILGRIM'S WAY

BY

HUMBERT WOLFE

1936

IVOR NICHOLSON AND WATSON
LIMITED . . . . LONDON

First published in 1936

PRINTED IN GREAT BRITAIN BY THE EDINBURGH PRESS, EDINBURGH AND LONDON

FOREWORD

IF this anthology has any value, and if when broadcast it had any success, only the smallest fraction of credit is mine. The original conception was Mr. Iremonger's—the Director of Religion of the British Broadcasting Corporation, and his share in the happy collaboration which extended over two years was greater than mine. Moreover, he would be the first to admit that both of us are under the greatest obligations to the musicians who matched the poems in the happiest marriage with melody of their own kind, to the successive producers and to the speakers—all of whom are listed below.

This much had to be said in mere honesty, lest when I briefly explain the underlying conception I might appear to claim it as my own. Mr. Iremonger's idea, then, was to illustrate the progress of man—the pilgrim of the world—through the varying moods, which are the milestones on the path from the cradle to the grave. It seemed to him that these moods could be projected by a combination of verse and music. He thought that in order to clinch the presentation it would be necessary to precede each broadcast with a brief prologue. If I would agree—as I enthusiastically did—he asked whether I would select the poems and write the prologue.

We started with the greatest zest. It was necessary to decide on the moods and their order. My first idea was to illustrate the progress from youth's hope and certainty through the doubts of adolescence, by way of the consummations of love, past the growing anguish and despair of later years to final peace when, at the end, all trouble is laid aside. This was well enough in theory: in practice it proved impossible. I had not considered the effect upon the British Broadcasting Corporation of a group of broadcasts successively and increasingly gloomy. By the time "Despair" was reached, Mr. Iremonger gently hinted, the emotion would be shared by the Directors of Broadcasting House. We had, therefore, to temper our Wolfe to the shorn lamb and gain in presentability what we lost in strict logic.

The general idea of the first year's series once settled I was sent off to produce the material for the first broadcast. This, as the volume indicates, was "Hope." Mr. Iremonger had suggested that I should choose extracts in equal proportions of prose and verse. I kept a brave front when I fell in with this proposal. Lest I should be dismissed forthwith, I did not admit that my ignorance of suitable prose was colossal. I had, it was true, a certain lack of working knowledge of the Bible. I had read Thomas à Kempis, *The Little Flowers of St. Francis*, and Newman's *Apologia pro vitâ suâ*. For the rest the literature of devotion was a closed book to me. I promised myself desperately to read volumes of sermons, to read my Fine Edition of the *Apocrypha* and even to flutter through the five volumes of the *Zohar*, magnificently produced by the Soncino Press.

In fact I read no prose. I found that my lack of knowledge of verse was as deep as a Mendip mine. In a panic I concluded that the only two poems, which I could remember, were Wordsworth's "We are seven" and Jean Ingelow's "High Tide on the Lincolnshire Coast" (and I doubted whether I had got the right titles for either). I decided, therefore, to read through the Aldine edition of British poets, bound in

Bristol boards, which A. A. B. had given me years ago.
I began with two authors called Akenside and Beattie. I
read them with increasing bewilderment. They did write,
I thought, such atrocious rubbish. But I was not lightly
defeated. I read them till one of the Bristol boards fell off.

The reader of the *Anthology* will discover no trace of these
authors. In far other places did I find my treasures. The
point of importance for me was that as I read I became more
and more deeply enchanted by all that the more erudite had
known by instinct and by birth. I wrote out vast numbers
of poems, as Du Maurier wrote out "Bonjour Suzanne,"
for the mere pleasure of writing them. I sent the B.B.C.
a wad of some forty highly inappropriate poems, together
with a Prologue, which would have formed a reasonable
introduction to a history of the world in seven volumes.

A certain silence brooded over the B.B.C. in my regard.
Presently a hesitating and tactfully-worded letter arrived, sug-
gesting that a conference might help all of us. I will not
harry the reader by describing the affair. It is enough to say
that on my return home I wrote a new Prologue for a com-
pletely different set of poems. One point, however, I had
established. The producer—Miss Allen—after considering my
selection of poems indicated (with what I thought was a
shudder) that I had better leave prose alone.

" Tantae molis erat Romanam condere gentem." I listed
incessantly. Now and again as many as three of my original
selections were accepted. On occasions the Prologue was
passed in the first draft. Nevertheless, as month succeeded
month all of us knew exactly what we wanted and—more
importantly—as a result of streams of letters, what the listeners
wanted. The musicians, after initial irritation and despair

began to tolerate me. All was set for calm when a mastoid operation intervened. This involved only one interruption. Mr. Ellis Roberts stepped into the breach and chose "Fear." I can only hope that the intervention of a more practised hand is not indicated by internal evidence.

Came the end of the year and to my delight an invitation to continue the series for a further year at bi-monthly intervals. In so far as there had been an original sequence of moods this had now frankly to be abandoned. But we consoled ourselves by reflecting that the pilgrim's moods were as many as a June's roses. We could, if invited, carry him on for another ten years. The B.B.C. were indulgent but not crazy. The great gong was sounded—and here at the end of two years are the results.

It remains only to chronicle all those other than Mr. Iremonger to whom the thanks of those who feel grateful are due. The names of the producers and speakers are contained in the list of the music attached at the end of each broadcast. In addition to all those whose collaboration was as valuable as it was enthusiastically given, there should be specially mentioned the unceasing supervision and help given by Sir Walford Davies, Mr. H. Foster Clark and Mr. Maurice Brown.

ACKNOWLEDGEMENTS

WE wish to thank the following who have kindly given permission for copyright poems to be used in this book:

The Author's executors and Messrs. Macmillan for " Frolic " from *The Collected Poems of A. E.*

Mr. Martin Armstrong and Messrs. Martin Secker & Warburg for an extract from *Grey*.

The Hon. Maurice Baring and Messrs. Heinemann for an extract from *In Memoriam to A. H.*

Mr. Gordon Bottomley and Messrs. Constable for " Night and Morning Songs."

The Author's executors and the Clarendon Press, Oxford, for " Youth," " Nightingales," " I Never Shall Love the Snow Again," and " Awake my Heart," by Robert Bridges.

Messrs. Sidgwick & Jackson, on behalf of the Author's executors, for " Busy Heart," by Rupert Brooke.

Mr. G. K. Chesterton and Messrs. Burns, Oates & Washbourne for " Lepanto " and " The Deluge " from *Collected Poems*, and " A Second Childhood " from *The Ballad of St. Barbara*.

Mr. G. K. Chesterton and Messrs. J. M. Dent for " By the Babe Unborn " and " The Donkey."

Mr. W. H. Davies for " Happy Child " and " Leisure."

Mrs. J. E. Flecker and Messrs. Martin Secker & Warburg for an extract from " Old Ships " and " Stillness " from *The Collected Poems of James Elroy Flecker*.

Mrs. Gertrude Freeman for " It was the Lovely Moon," by John Freeman.

Mr. H. W. Garrod for " The Garden."

Mr. Gerald Gould and Messrs. Victor Gollancz for " Oxford."

Lord Desborough for " Into Battle," by Julian Grenfell.

Mrs. Thomas Hardy for " Waiting Both " and " When I Set Out for Lyonesse," by Thomas Hardy.

The Author's executors and Messrs. Macmillan for " Invictus," by W. E. Henley.

Mr. Ralph Hodgson and Messrs. Macmillan for an extract from " Song of Honour," " Eve," and " Mystery " from *The Poems of Ralph Hodgson.*

The Author's executors and The Oxford University Press for " Pied Beauty " and " Starlight Night," by Gerard Manly Hopkins.

Mr. Shane Leslie for " Fleet Street."

Miss Rose Macaulay for " Recovery."

Mr. Walter de la Mare and Messrs. James B. Pinker & Son for " Futility " and " Scribe."

Mr. John Masefield and Messrs. Heinemann for " Sea-Fever," " Seekers," " His Mother," and " Invocation " from *The Collected Poems of John Masefield.*

Mr. Wilfrid Meynell and Messrs Burns, Oates & Washbourne for " To a Daisy " and an extract from " Christ in the Universe," by Alice Meynell.

Mr. Humphrey Milford and The Oxford University Press for extracts from the Revised Version of the Bible.

Mrs. F. W. H. Myers and Messrs. Macmillan for an extract from " The Implicit Promise of Immortality," by F. W. H. Myers.

The Author's executors and Messrs. Chatto & Windus for "The End," by Wilfrid Owen.

Mr. Herbert Palmer for "Joy" and "Prayer to the Virgin."

Mr. George Santayana and Messrs. Constable for "O World, Thou Choosest Not."

The Author's executors for "Comforters," by Dora Sigerson Shorter.

The Author's executors and the Cambridge University Press for "Song of the Ungirt Runners," by Charles Hamilton Sorley.

Mr. Stephen Spender and Messrs. Faber & Faber for "Moving through the Silent Crowd" from *The Poems of Stephen Spender*.

Mr. James Stephens and Messrs. Macmillan for "April Showers," "Snare," and an extract from "The Seeker" from *The Collected Poems of James Stephens*.

Mr. Arthur Symons and Messrs. Heinemann for "Montserrat."

Mrs. Helen Thomas for an extract from "Trumpets" and an extract from "Lights Out," by Edward Thomas.

Mr. Edward Thompson for his translation of "They Have All Gone to the Woods," by Rabindranath Tagore.

Mr. Wilfrid Meynell and Messrs. Burns, Oates & Washbourne for "Kingdom of God," "Snowflake," and an extract from "The Hound of Heaven," by Francis Thompson.

Mr. W. J. Turner for "Ecstasy" and "Princess."

Mr. Louis Untermeyer and Messrs. Harcourt Brace for "Prayer."

Mr. V. B. Holland for an extract from "The Ballad of Reading Gaol," by Oscar Wilde.

Mr. W. B. Yeats and Messrs. Macmillan for "The Fiddler of Dooney" and "That the Night Came" from *The Collected Poems of W. B. Yeats.*

In a few cases where it has been impossible to obtain permission to reproduce certain poems, others have been substituted for those originally used in the Broadcast.

CONTENTS

PART I—HOPE

PART II—FAITH

PART III—JOY

PART IV—DOUBT

CONTENTS

PART V—LOVE

PART VI—CONTEMPLATION

XV

PART VII—FEAR

PART VIII—COURAGE

PART IX—SORROW

CONTENTS

PART X—TEMPTATION

PART XI—WORSHIP

PART XII—EXPECTATION

PART XIII—CONTRITION

PART XIV—ASSURANCE

CONTENTS

PART XVII—PEACE

PART ONE

HOPE

A

Producer:

Miss M. H. ALLEN.

Speakers:

NATALIE MOYA.

ION SWINLEY.

JOHN CHEATLE.

Music:

Selected by H. FOSTER CLARK.

Quartet in G Major, Op. 20, No. 2 (Haydn), 2nd, 3rd and 4th Movements.   H.M.V. DB1629.

Quartet in G Minor, Op. 74, No. 3 (Haydn), 1st and 2nd Movements.   H.M.V. DB1632.

Quartet in C Major, Op. 33, No. 3 (Haydn), 3rd and 4th Movements.   H.M.V. DB1631.

Nunc Dimittis.   Columbia 5711.

Quartet in A (Armstrong Gibbs), 3rd Movement.

H.M.V. B4452.

Tantum Ergo (Traditional).   Columbia 4969.

PROLOGUE

THIS is an age of turmoil, doubt and exhaustion. In such ages—and there have been such ages after every great war—men become disillusioned and look everywhere for comfort and restoration except to the old and simple truths. They see life as a series of confused struggles with no particular origin and no defined aim. There is movement furious enough but, as men think, without direction. They forget—and if reminded, mock at the plain fact—that today, as always, in spite of fog, darkness or sorrow, life is a pilgrimage such as was greatly described by John Bunyan; that we are all, from the day of our birth to the last day of all, pilgrims on the Pilgrim's Way. We suffer the same moods and emotions as did our fathers before us, and as will our children after us. Though we give them the old names they are none the less new for each one of us. Each man's moods and emotions are private, different, and utterly his own.

We are attempting here to illustrate for you, through poetry and music, one man's pilgrimage, though, by happy accident, it may well be that of many. The milestones that we have set up on the way are those that the poets and the musicians have left for us.

Tonight, we draw the curtain of the first scene of our chronicle and display the pilgrim dabbling with bright fingers in the pools of Hope.

3

Pippa's Song

The year's at the spring,
And day's at the morn;
Morning's at seven;
The hill-side's dew-pearl'd;
The lark's on the wing;
The snail's on the thorn;
God's in His heaven—
All's right with the world!

ROBERT BROWNING.

[*Music*]

Frolic

The children were shouting together
    And racing along the sands,
A glimmer of dancing shadows,
    A dovelike flutter of hands.

The stars were shouting in heaven,
    The sun was chasing the moon:
The game was the same as the children's,
    They danced to the self-same tune.

The whole of the world was merry,
    One joy from the vale to the height,
Where the blue woods of twilight encircled
    The lovely lawns of the light.

A. E.

[*Music*]

Reeds of Innocence

Piping down the valleys wild,
    Piping songs of pleasant glee,
On a cloud I saw a child,
    And he laughing said to me:

5

" Pipe a song about a Lamb ! "
  So I piped with merry cheer.
" Piper, pipe that song again " ;
  So I piped : he wept to hear.

" Drop thy pipe, thy happy pipe ;
  Sing thy songs of happy cheer ! "
So I sung the same again,
  While he wept with joy to hear.

" Piper, sit thee down and write,
  In a book that I may read."
So he vanish'd from my sight ;
  And I pluck'd a hollow reed,

And I made a rural pen,
  And I stain'd the water clear,
And I wrote my happy songs
  Every child may joy to hear.

WILLIAM BLAKE.

[*Music*]

A Child's Grace

Here a little child I stand
Heaving up my either hand ;
Cold as paddocks though they be,
Here I lift them up to Thee,
For a benison to fall
On our meat and on us all. AMEN.

ROBERT HERRICK.

[*Music*]

6

The Happy Child

I saw this day sweet flowers grow thick—
But not one like the child did pick.

I heard the packhounds in green park—
But no dog like the child heard bark.

I heard this day bird after bird—
But not one like the child has heard.

A hundred butterflies saw I—
But not one like the child saw fly.

I saw the horses roll in grass—
But no horse like the child saw pass.

My world this day has lovely been—
But not what like the child has seen.

W. H. DAVIES.

[*Music*]

Ode on Intimations of Immortality

O joy! that in our embers
Is something that doth live,
That nature yet remembers
What was so fugitive!
The thought of our past years in me doth breed
Perpetual benediction: not indeed
For that which is most worthy to be blest—
Delight and liberty, the simple creed
Of childhood, whether busy or at rest,
With new-fledged hope still fluttering in his breast:—
Not for these I raise
The song of thanks and praise;

7

But for those obstinate questionings
Of sense and outward things,
Fallings from us, vanishings;
Blank misgivings of a Creature
Moving about in worlds not realized,
High instincts before which our mortal Nature
Did tremble like a guilty thing surprised:
But for those first affections,
Those shadowy recollections,
Which, be they what they may,
Are yet the fountain light of all our day,
Are yet a master-light of all our seeing;
Uphold us, cherish, and have power to make
Our noisy years seem moments in the being
Of the eternal Silence: truths that wake,
To perish never:
Which neither listlessness, nor mad endeavour,
Nor Man nor Boy,
Nor all that is at enmity with joy,
Can utterly abolish or destroy!
Hence in a season of calm weather
Though inland far we be,
Our souls have sight of that immortal sea
Which brought us hither
Can in a moment travel thither,
And see the children sport upon the shore,
And hear the mighty waters rolling evermore.

WILLIAM WORDSWORTH.

[*Music*]

Isaiah xxxv.

The wilderness and the solitary place shall be glad for them; and the desert shall rejoice, and blossom as the rose.

It shall blossom abundantly, and rejoice even with joy and singing: the glory of Lebanon shall be given unto it, the excellency of Carmel and Sharon, they shall see the glory of the Lord, and the excellency of our God.

Strengthen ye the weak hands, and confirm the feeble knees.

Say to them that are of a fearful heart, Be strong, fear not: behold, your God will come with vengeance, even God with a recompence; he will come and save you.

Then the eyes of the blind shall be opened, and the ears of the deaf shall be unstopped.

Then shall the lame man leap as an hart, and the tongue of the dumb sing: for in the wilderness shall waters break out, and streams in the desert.

And the parched ground shall become a pool, and the thirsty land springs of water: in the habitation of dragons, where each lay, shall be grass with reeds and rushes.

And an highway shall be there, and a way, and it shall be called The way of holiness; the unclean shall not pass over it; but it shall be for those: the wayfaring men, though fools, shall not err therein.

No lion shall be there, nor any ravenous beast shall go up thereon, it shall not be found there; but the redeemed shall walk there:

And the ransomed of the Lord shall return, and come to Zion with songs and everlasting joy upon their heads: they shall obtain joy and gladness, and sorrow and sighing shall flee away.

[*Music*]

9

Ecstasy

I saw a frieze on whitest marble drawn
Of boys who sought for shells along the shore,
Their white feet shedding pallor in the sea,
The shallow sea, the spring-time sea of green
That faintly creamed against the cold, smooth pebbles. . . .

One held a shell unto his shell-like ear
And there was music carven in his face,
His eyes half-closed, his lips just breaking open
To catch the lulling, mazy coralline roar
Of numberless caverns filled with singing seas.

And all of them were hearkening as to singing
Of far-off voices thin and delicate,
Voices too fine for any mortal wind
To blow into the whorls of mortal ears—
And yet those sounds flowed from their grave sweet faces.

And as I looked I heard that delicate music,
And I became as grave, as calm, as still
As those carved boys. I stood upon that shore,
I felt the cool sea dream around my feet,
My eyes were staring at the far horizon. . . .

WALTER J. TURNER.

[Music]

Romance

I will make you brooches and toys for your delight
Of bird-song at morning and star-shine at night.
I will make a palace fit for you and me,
Of green days in forests and blue days at sea.

I will make my kitchen, and you shall keep your room,
Where white flows the river and bright blows the broom,
And you shall wash your linen and keep your body white
In rainfall at morning and dewfall at night.

And this shall be for music when no one else is near,
The fine song for singing, the rare song to hear!
That only I remember, that only you admire,
Of the broad road that stretches and the roadside fire.

ROBERT LOUIS STEVENSON.

[*Music*]

Into Spring

Into spring
Whispering
" O " there ran
My daughter Ann.

HUMBERT WOLFE.

[*Music*]

They Have all Gone to the Woods

They have all gone to the woods in this moonlit night,
In the south wind drunken with Spring's delight.
    But I will not go, will not go;
    I will stay in the house, and so
Wait in my lonely corner—this night
I will not go in this south wind drunk with delight.

Rather this room with care
I must scour and cleanse and prepare;
    For . . . if He remembers me, then
    He will come, though I know not when;
They must wake me swiftly. I will not fare
Out where the drunk wind reels through the air.

RABINDRANATH TAGORE.

[*Music*]

Psalm cxxi.

I will lift up mine eyes unto the hills, from whence cometh my help.

My help cometh from the Lord, which made heaven and earth.

He will not suffer thy foot to be moved: he that keepeth thee will not slumber.

Behold, he that keepeth Israel shall neither slumber nor sleep.

The Lord is thy keeper: the Lord is thy shade upon thy right hand.

The sun shall not smite thee by day, nor the moon by night.

The Lord shall preserve thee from all evil: he shall preserve thy soul.

The Lord shall preserve thy going out and thy coming in from this time forth, and even for evermore.

[*Music*]

The Trumpet

Rise up, rise up,
And, as the trumpet blowing
Chases the dreams of men,
As the dawn glowing
The stars that left unlit
The land and water,
Rise up and scatter
The dew that covers
The print of last night's lovers—
Scatter it, scatter it!

While you are listening
To the clear horn,
Forget, men, everything
On this earth newborn,
Except that it is lovelier
Than any mysteries.
Open your eyes to the air
That has washed the eyes of the stars
Through all the dewy night:
Up with the light,
To the old wars;
Arise, arise!

EDWARD THOMAS.

[*Finale*]

PART TWO

FAITH

Producer:
Miss M. H. ALLEN.

Speakers:
DENNIS ARUNDELL.
RICHARD AINLEY.
[*By kind permission of Miss Lilian Baylis.*]

Music:
Selected by H. FOSTER CLARK.

Symphony No. 1 (Elgar), 1st Movement.
                                    H.M.V. D1944.
Symphony No. 1 (Elgar), 1st Movement.
                                    H.M.V. D1945.
Symphony No. 1 (Elgar), 3rd Movement.
                                    H.M.V. D1947.
Prelude in E Flat Minor (Bach).   H.M.V. D1464.
First Symphony (Brahms), 2nd and 3rd Movements.
                                    H.M.V. D1456.
Concerto, No. 5 (Beethoven), 2nd Movement.
                                    H.M.V. D1200.
" The Kingdom," Prelude (Elgar).   H.M.V. DB1934.
" Jerusalem " (Blake and Parry).   Columbia 9763.

PROLOGUE

THE first milestone on the way is Hope, the second Faith. The pilgrim has been aware of life rising in his veins urgent as sap. Hope is the name of that first impulse—the time of young leaves. As the leaves uncrumple the first wild surmise is confirmed. " I think, therefore I am," said a greater thinker. " I can, therefore I will," says Faith. For Faith is the belief that man can and will prevail first upon himself and then upon the world. Youth has heard rumours of failure. He carries, he knows, in his body the inherited seed of disaster. It does not matter. He will succeed the better for difficulty. He is warned that life lies in wait for him like a footpad at the side of the road. He will snatch the weapon and use it against the aggressor. I am, says youth, therefore I can. Because I can, I shall bend the mountains.

The world can be re-moulded to the movement of a song or shaped in the brave outline of dream. All men are poets in the moment of Faith : for all there is the instant when the dream dictates to reality. Nor does poem or dream falter because the world is dark and shaken. The further for darkness will that private torch throw its beam. Nor will it be solitary. Torch will answer torch of the regiment of Faith pledged in a conspiracy to carry standards through the night.

They do not march without guidance. If Faith in self and in the future are the captains, the general is still the Faith in God, illuminating and instructing both with its ancient certainties.

There has always been in the mind of man the urgent wish to reach out beyond himself to that which is flawless when he is flawed, bright when he walks in shadow and timeless when he faces death. The pitiful wood of the savage idol is no less than St. Peter's Church in Rome the consecration of this universal belief and need. The pilgrim has Faith in himself for himself, but still more because he is the instrument of God. He has Faith in the future, because he believes that he can mould it, but first and chiefly because he is working to a plan beyond his own conception, of which the bright outline glimmers upon him in moments of ecstasy.

Forward, therefore, pilgrim, in Faith. Joy waits with his long trumpets a little further on.

" O World, Thou Choosest Not "

O World, thou choosest not the better part!
It is not wisdom to be only wise,
And on the inward vision close the eyes,
But it is wisdom to believe the heart.
Columbus found a world, and had no chart,
Save one that faith deciphered in the skies;
To trust the soul's invincible surmise
Was all his science and his only art.
Our knowledge is a torch of smoky pine
That lights the pathway but one step ahead
Across a void of mystery and dread.
Bid, then, the tender light of faith to shine
By which alone the mortal heart is led
Unto the thinking of the thought divine.

GEORGE SANTAYANA.

[*Music*]

Ode

We are the music-makers,
  And we are the dreamers of dreams,
Wandering by lone sea-breakers,
  And sitting by desolate streams;
World losers and world forsakers,
  On whom the pale moon gleams:
Yet we are the movers and shakers
  Of the world for ever, it seems.

With wonderful deathless ditties
We build up the world's great cities;
  And out of a fabulous story
  We fashion an empire's glory:

One man with a dream, at pleasure,
   Shall go forth and conquer a crown;
And three with a new song's measure
   Can trample an empire down.

We, in the ages lying
   In the buried past of the earth,
Built Nineveh with our sighing,
   And Babel itself with our mirth;
And o'erthrew them with prophesying
   To the old of the new world's worth;
For each age is a dream that is dying,
   Or one that is coming to birth.

ARTHUR O'SHAUGHNESSY.

[*Music*]

In Memoriam

Love is and was my Lord and King,
   And in his presence I attend
   To hear the tidings of my friend,
Which every hour his couriers bring.

Love is and was my King and Lord,
   And will be, tho' as yet I keep
   Within his court on earth, and sleep
Encompass'd by his faithful guard.

And hear at times a sentinel
   Who moves about from place to place,
   And whispers to the worlds of space,
In the deep night, that all is well.

TENNYSON.

[*Music*]

" *I have seen* "

I have seen
A curious child, who dwelt upon a tract
Of inland ground, applying to his ear
The convolutions of a smooth-lipped shell;
To which, in silence hushed, his very soul
Listened intensely; and his countenance soon
Brightened with joy; for from within were heard
Murmurings, whereby the monitor expressed
Mysterious union with its native sea.
Even such a shell the universe itself
Is to the ear of Faith; and there are times,
I doubt not, when to you it doth impart
Authentic tidings of invisible things;
Of ebb and flow, and ever-during power;
And central peace, subsisting at the heart
Of endless agitation.

WILLIAM WORDSWORTH.

[*Music*]

Psalm cxxxix. 1–12

O Lord, thou hast searched me, and known me.

Thou knowest my downsitting and mine uprising,
Thou understandest my thought afar off.

Thou searchest out my path and my lying down,
And art acquainted with all my ways.

For there is not a word in my tongue,
But, lo, O Lord, thou knowest it altogether.

Thou hast beset me behind and before
And laid thine hand upon me.

Such knowledge is too wonderful for me;
It is high, I cannot attain unto it.

Whither shall I go from thy spirit?
Or whither shall I flee from thy presence?

If I ascend up into heaven thou art there:
If I make my bed in Sheol, behold, thou art there.

If I take the wings of the morning,
And dwell in the uttermost parts of the sea;

Even there shall thy hand lead me,
And thy right hand shall hold me.

If I say, surely the darkness shall overwhelm me,
And the light about me shall be night;

Even the darkness hideth not from thee,
But the night shineth as the day:
The darkness and the light are both alike to thee.

[*Music*]

Resurrection and Immortality

BODY

Oft have I seen, when that renewing breath
    That binds and loosens death
Inspir'd a quickening power through the dead
    creatures a-bed.

    Some drowsie silk-worme creepe
        from that long sleepe
And in weake, infant hummings chime, and knell
        About her silent cell.

22

Untill at last full with the vitall Ray
   she wing'd away,
 And proud with life, and sence
   Heaven's rich expence.

Esteem'd (vaine things!) of two whole elements
   As meane, and span-extents.
Shall I then thinke such providence will be
   Lesse friend to me?

Or that he can endure to be unjust
Who keeps his Covenant even with the dust.

HENRY VAUGHAN.

   [*Music*]

England 1802

O Friend! I know not which way I must look
 For comfort, being, as I am opprest,
To think that now our life is only drest
For show; mean handy-work of craftsman, cook,
Or groom!—We must run glittering like a brook
 In the open sunshine, or we are unblest:
 The wealthiest man among us is the best:
No grandeur now in nature or in book
Delights us. Rapine, avarice, expense,
 This is idolatry; and these we adore:
 Plain living and high thinking are no more:
 The homely beauty of the good old cause
Is gone; our peace, our fearful innocence,
 And pure religion breathing household laws.

WILLIAM WORDSWORTH.

   [*Music*]

Say not the Struggle naught availeth

Say not the struggle nought availeth,
   The labour and the wounds are vain,
The enemy faints not, nor faileth,
   And as things have been they remain.

If hopes were dupes, fears may be liars;
   It may be, in yon smoke conceal'd,
Your comrades chase e'en now the fliers,
   And, but for you, possess the field.

For while the tired waves, vainly breaking,
   Seem here no painful inch to gain,
Far back, through creeks and inlets making,
   Comes silent, flooding in, the main.

And not by eastern windows only,
   When daylight comes, comes in the light;
In front, the sun climbs slow, how slowly,
   But westward, look, the land is bright.

ARTHUR HUGH CLOUGH.

[*Music*]

From " Riding Westward "

I am carryed towards the West
This day, when my Soules forme bends toward the
   East.
There I should see a Sunne, by rising set,
And by that setting endless day beget;
But that Christ on this Crosse, did rise and fall,
Sinne had eternally benighted all.

24

Yet dare I'almost be glad, I do not see
That spectacle of too much weight for mee.
Who sees God's face, that is self life, must dye;
What a death were it then to see God dye?
It made his owne Lieutenant Nature shrinke,
It made his footstoole crack, and the Sunne winke.
Could I behold those hands which span the Poles,
And turne all spheares at once, pierc'd with those
    holes?
Could I behold that endless height which is
Zenith to us, and our Antipodes,
Humbled below us? or that blood which is
The seat of all our Soules, if not of his,
Made durt of dust, or that flesh which was worne
By God, for his apparell, rag'd, and torne?
If on these things I durst not looke, durst I
Upon his miserable mother cast mine eye,
Who was God's partner here, and furnish'd thus
Halfe of that Sacrifice, which ransom'd us?
Though these things, as I ride, be from mine eye.
They'are present yet unto my memory,
For that looks towards them; and thou look'st to-
    wards mee,
O Saviour, as thou hang'st upon the tree;
I turne my backe to thee, but to receive
Corrections, till thy mercies bid thee leave.
O thinke mee worth thine anger, punish mee,
Burne off my rusts, and my deformity,
Restore thine Image, so much, by thy grace,
That thou may'st know mee, and I'll turne my face.

JOHN DONNE.

[Music]

25

To God

Make, make me Thine, my gracious God,
Or with thy staffe, or with thy rod;
And be the blow too what it will,
Lord I will kisse it, though it kill;
Beat me, bruise me, rack me, rend me,
Yet, in torments, I'le commend Thee:
Nor shalt Thou give so deep a wound,
But I as patient will be found.

ROBERT HERRICK.

[*Music*]

Isaiah xl. 27–31

Why sayest thou, O Jacob, and speakest, O Israel, My way is hid from the Lord, and my judgement is passed away from my God?

Hast thou not known? hast thou not heard? the everlasting God, the Lord, the Creator of the ends of the earth, fainteth not, neither is weary; there is no searching of his understanding.

He giveth power to the faint; and to him that hath no might He increaseth strength.

Even the youths shall faint and be weary, and the young men shall utterly fall:

But they that wait upon the Lord shall renew their strength; they shall mount up with wings as eagles; they shall run and not be weary; they shall walk and not faint.

[*Music*]

26

The Kingdom of God

O world invisible, we view thee,
O world intangible, we touch thee,
O world unknowable, we know thee,
Inapprehensible, we clutch thee!

Does the fish soar to find the ocean,
The eagle plunge to find the air—
That we ask of the stars in motion
If they have rumour of thee there?

Not where the wheeling systems darken,
And our benumbed conceiving soars!
The drift of pinions, would we hearken,
Beats at our own clay-shuttered doors.

The angels keep their ancient places;—
Turn but a stone, and start a wing!
'Tis ye, 'tis your estrangèd faces,
That miss the many-splendoured thing.

But (when so sad thou canst not sadder)
Cry;—and upon thy so sore loss
Shall shine the traffic of Jacob's ladder
Pitched betwixt Heaven and Charing Cross.

Yea, in the night, my Soul, my daughter,
Cry,—clinging Heaven by the hems;
And lo, Christ walking on the water
Not of Gennesareth, but Thames!

FRANCIS THOMPSON.

[Music]

27

Jerusalem

And did those feet in ancient time
  Walk upon England's mountains green?
And was the holy Lamb of God
  On England's pleasant pastures seen?
And did the countenance divine
  Shine forth upon our clouded hills?
And was Jerusalem builded here
  Among those dark satanic mills?

Bring me my bow of burning gold!
  Bring me my arrows of desire!
Bring me my spear! O clouds, unfold!
  Bring me my chariot of fire!
I will not cease from mental fight,
  Nor shall my sword sleep in my hand,
Till we have built Jerusalem
  In England's green and pleasant land.

WILLIAM BLAKE.

[*Music*]

Youth

O Youth whose hope is high,
Who dost to Truth aspire,
Whether thou live or die,
O look not back nor tire.

Thou that art bold to fly
Through tempest, flood and fire,
Nor dost not shrink to try
Thy heart in torments dire:

If thou canst Death defy,
If thy Faith is entire,
Press onward, for thine eye
Shall see thy heart's desire.

Beauty and love are nigh,
And with their deathless quire
Soon shall thine eager cry
Be numbered and expire.

ROBERT BRIDGES.

[*Music*]

PART THREE

JOY

Producer:

Miss M. H. ALLEN.

Speakers:

JANET TAYLOR.

ROBERT HARRIS.

DAVID TENNANT.

Music:

Selected by H. FOSTER CLARK.

" Oberon " (Weber), Overture.   H.M.V. D1311.

Symphony, No. 7 (Beethoven), in A Major, Op. 92,
    1st Movement.   H.M.V. D1639.

Symphony, No. 7 (Beethoven), 1st and 2nd Movements.
          H.M.V. D1640.

Symphony, No. 7 (Beethoven), 2nd Movement.
          H.M.V. D1641.

Symphony, No. 6 (Beethoven), in F Major, 3rd and
    4th Movements.   H.M.V. D1476.

Symphony, No. 6 (Beethoven), in F Major, 5th Move-
    ment.   H.M.V. D1477.

Enigma Variations (Elgar), (5, 6, 7, 8 and 9).
          H.M.V. D1155.

Suite, No. 3, in D Major (J. S. Bach), " Air."
          H.M.V. DB1964.

An Irish Symphony (Hamilton Harty), Scherzo.
          Columbia 9891.

PROLOGUE

JOY is to be aware of life. The pilgrim has hoped and believed, now at a stride he has stepped out of the happy shadow into the complete sun. Like a child unborn he has trembled on the threshold, searching for the door and beating upon it with doubtful hands. Suddenly it is flung wide, and, a child released from the darkness of school, he rushes shouting into his inheritance of light. He embraces the vigour of life in friendship and in the growth of soul that shared experience gives. There are no lessons more to be learned save at the knees of the source of life. Everybody has burst out singing.

With that huge merriment when the sun shakes his side like Falstaff and the moon laughs as clear as a silver sixpence, the pilgrim is off to the greenwood where among trees all being is subdued to a green thought in a green shade. Here are flowers and the dancing daffodils. Here is bird-song— the nightingale bright from fruitful valleys and the blackbird who bewitches childhood and rings at Peter's gate in heaven. But bird-song bids the pilgrim remember flute, fiddle and the measures of the dance. On upland pasture and on the broad green turf he steps out gaily and hears the fiddler whose violin calls with the rhythm of the wave.

Joy is restless. The fiddle and the dancing invite the pilgrim to the distance and the motion of the sea. The road begs him of the greenwood and lends him to the ocean. There he rejoices in his strength and in his quest of " the bright eyes of danger."

There is Joy on the way out. There is another and as deep a Joy on the homeward road. For every pilgrim in all adventure at the end of the journey wait his native town and his native dream. England for the English, Rome for the Roman, but for all their own town and their own place, the more beloved because it has dwindled to a charm small enough to hang round the neck above the heart.

And here by his own hearth again the pilgrim tells over to himself what he has known and shared in the danger of beauty. The birds that sang, and the flowers that danced before him have become a part of his mind in tranquillity. The inner significance of joy becomes greatly apparent. It has become a thing of beauty. It rises in shawn and psaltery to the steps of the Throne.

From " By the Babe Unborn "

I think that if they gave me leave
   Within the world to stand,
I would be good through all the day
   I spent in fairyland.

They should not hear a word from me
   Of selfishness or scorn,
If only I could find the door,
   If only I were born.

G. K. CHESTERTON.

[Music]

April Showers

The leaves are fresh after the rain.
The air is cool and clear,
The sun is shining warm again
The sparrows hopping in the lane
Are brisk and full of cheer.

And that is why we dance and play,
And that is why we sing,
Calling out in voices gay,
We will not go to school to-day
Nor learn anything.

It is a happy thing, I say,
To be alive on such a day.

JAMES STEPHENS.

[Music]

Everyone suddenly burst out Singing

Everyone suddenly burst out singing:
And I was filled with such delight
As prisoned birds must find in freedom,
Winging wilding across the white
Orchards and dark-green fields; on—on—and out
    out of sight.

Everyone's voice was suddenly lifted:
And beauty came like the setting sun;
My heart was shaken with tears; and horror
Drifted away— . . . O but—everyone
Was a bird; and the song was wordless: the singing
    will never be done.

SIEGFRIED SASSOON.

[Music]

From " Saul "

" Oh, our manhood's prime vigour." No spirit feels waste,
Not a muscle is stopped in its playing nor sinew unbraced.
Oh, the wild joys of living! the leaping from rock up to rock,
The strong rending of boughs from the fir-tree, the cool
    silver shock
Of the plunge in a pool's living water, the hunt of the bear,
And the sultriness showing the lion is couched in his lair.
And the meal, the rich dates yellowed over with gold dust divine,
And the locust-flesh steeped in the pitcher, the full draught
    of wine,
And the sleep in the dried river channel where bulrushes tell
That the water was wont to go warbling so softly and well,
How good is man's life, the mere living! how fit to employ
All the heart and the soul and the senses for ever in joy!

ROBERT BROWNING.

[Music]

I *Wandered Lonely as a Cloud*

I wandered lonely as a cloud
That floats on high o'er vales and hills,
When all at once I saw a crowd,
A host, of golden daffodils;
Beside the lake, beneath the trees,
Fluttering and dancing in the breeze.

Continuous as the stars that shine
And twinkle on the milky way,
They stretched in never-ending line
Along the margin of a bay:
Ten thousand saw I at a glance,
Tossing their heads in sprightly dance.

The waves beside them danced; but they
Out-did the sparkling waves in glee;
A poet could not but be gay,
In such a jocund company:
I gazed—and gazed—but little thought
What wealth the show to me had brought:

For oft, when on my couch I lie
In vacant or in pensive mood,
They flash upon that inward eye
Which is the bliss of solitude;
And then my heart with pleasure fills,
And dances with the daffodils.

WILLIAM WORDSWORTH.

[*Music*]

37

Nightingales

Beautiful must be the mountains whence ye come,
And bright in the fruitful valleys the streams, wherefrom
      Ye learn your song:
Where are those starry woods? O might I wander there,
    Among the flowers, which in that heavenly air
      Bloom the year long!

Nay, barren are those mountains and spent the streams:
Our song is the voice of desire, that haunts our dreams,
      A throe of the heart,
Whose pining visions dim, forbidden hopes profound,
    No dying cadence nor long sigh can sound,
      For all our art.

Alone, aloud in the raptured ear of men
We pour our dark nocturnal secret; and then,
      As night is withdrawn
From these sweet-springing meads and bursting boughs of May,
    Dream, while the innumerable choir of day
      Welcome the dawn.

                ROBERT BRIDGES.

    [*Music*]

The Blackbird

In the far corner
  close by the swings
every morning
  a blackbird sings.
His bill's so yellow,
  his coat's so black
that he makes a fellow
  answer back.

38

Ann my daughter
thinks that he
sings for us two
especially.

HUMBERT WOLFE.

[*Music*]

Magdalen

Magdalen at Michael's gate
    Tirlèd at the pin;
On Joseph's thorn sang the blackbird,
    " Let her in! Let her in! "

" Hast thou seen the wounds? " said Michael,
    " Know'st thou thy sin? "
" It is evening, evening," sang the blackbird,
    " Let her in! Let her in! "

" Yes, I have seen the wounds,
    And I know my sin."
" She knows it well, well, well," sang the blackbird,
    " Let her in! Let her in! "

" Thou bringest no offerings," said Michael.
    " Nought save sin."
And the blackbird sang, " She is sorry, sorry, sorry,
    " Let her in! Let her in! "

When he had sung himself to sleep,
    And night did begin,
One came and open'd Michael's gate,
    And Magdalen went in.

HENRY KINGSLEY.

[*Music*]

L'Allegro

Sometimes, with secure delight,
The upland hamlets will invite,
When the merry bells ring round
And the jocund rebecks sound
To many a youth and many a maid
Dancing in the checkered shade,
And young and old come forth to play
On a sunshine holyday,
Till the livelong daylight fail;
Then to the spicy nut-brown ale,
With stories told of many a feat;
How fairy Mab the junkets eat;
She was pinched, and pulled, she said;
And he, by friar's lantern led,
Tells how the drudging goblin sweat
To earn his cream-bowl duly set,
When, in one night, ere glimpse of morn,
His shadowy flail hath threshed the corn
That ten day labourers could not end;
Then lies him down the lubber fiend,
And, stretched out all the chimney's length
Basks at the fire his hairy strength,
And crop-full, out of doors he flings,
Ere the first cock his matin rings.
Thus done the tales, to bed they creep,
By whispering winds soon lulled asleep.

JOHN MILTON.

[*Music*]

40

Joy

Some men have died for Religion,
And some for a Soldier's Cause,
The poet for Vision and Beauty,
Strong Statesmen to better Earth's Laws.
But sound for me now lute and timbrel
That my singing be cleansed from alloy;
I would lay down my life for the crown of them all,
Oh, I would die for Joy!

I have wooed fair Joy in the twilight
'Neath the sweep of a glimmering sword,
I have crept like a thief through the dark night
And plundered her starry hoard.
The wings of her spirit have risen
From the foam of the Dead Sea swell,
And my soul has breathed free from its prison
When I suffered what tongue could not tell.

Oh, lend me some Weapon of Wonder
To fight for this spirit of Might!
I would cleave the dark storm-clouds asunder
And bring the Earth stars of delight.
Let me stand with my face to her Slayer
And fall where Death's legions deploy,
But ne'er by weak living betray her,
Brave Joy, radiant Joy.

HERBERT PALMER.

[Music]

41

The Fiddler of Dooney

When I play on my fiddle in Dooney
    Folk dance like a wave of the sea;
My cousin is priest at Kilvarnet
    My brother in Moharabuiee.

I passed my brother and cousin;
    They read in their books of prayer;
I read in my books of songs
    I bought at Sligo fair.

When we come to the end of time,
    To Peter sitting in state,
He will smile on the three old spirits,
    But call me first through the gate.

For the good are always the merry,
    Save by an evil chance;
And the merry love the fiddle
    And the merry love to dance.

And when the folk there spy me,
    They will all come up to me,
With " Here is the fiddler of Dooney,"
    And dance like a wave of the sea.

W. B. YEATS.

[*Music*]

Sea-Fever

I must down to the seas again, to the lonely sea and the sky,
And all I ask is a tall ship and a star to steer her by,
And the wheel's kick and the wind's song and the white sail's
    shaking,
And a grey mist on the sea's face and a grey dawn breaking.

I must down to the seas again, for the call of the running tide,
Is a wild call and a clear call that may not be denied;
And all I ask is a windy day with the white clouds flying,
And the flung spray and the blown spume, and the sea-gulls
    crying.

I must down to the seas again, to the vagrant gypsy life,
To the gull's way and the whale's way where the wind's like
    a whetted knife;
And all I ask is a merry yarn from a laughing fellow-rover,
And a quiet sleep and a sweet dream when the long trick's over.

JOHN MASEFIELD.

[Music]

Home-thoughts, from Abroad

O, to be in England
Now that April's there,
And whoever wakes in England
Sees, some morning, unaware,
That the lowest boughs and the brushwood sheaf
Round the elm-tree bole are in tiny leaf,
While the chaffinch sings on the orchard bough
In England—now!

And after April, when May follows,
And the whitethroat builds, and all the swallows!
Hark, where my blossom'd pear-tree in the hedge
Leans to the field and scatters on the clover
Blossoms and dewdrops—at the bent spray's edge—
That's the wise thrush; he sings each song twice over,

43

Lest you should think he never could recapture
The first fine careless rapture!
And though the fields look rough with hoary dew,
All will be gay when noontide wakes anew
The buttercups, the little children's dower
—Far brighter than this gaudy-melon-flower!

ROBERT BROWNING.

[*Music*]

The Poet's Dream

On a poet's lips I slept
Dreaming like a love-adept
In the sound his breathing kept;
Nor seeks nor finds he mortal blisses
But feeds on the aerial kisses
Of shapes that haunt Thought's wildernesses.
He will watch from dawn to gloom
The lake-reflected sun illume
The yellow bee in the ivy-bloom,
Nor heed nor see what things they be—
But from these create he can
Forms more real than living man
Nurslings of Immortality.

PERCY BYSSHE SHELLEY.

[*Music*]

From " Endymion "

A thing of beauty is a joy for ever:
Its loveliness increases; it will never
Pass into nothingness; but still will keep
A bower quite for us, and a sleep

44

Full of sweet dreams, and health, and quiet breathing.
Therefore on every morrow, are we wreathing
A flowery band to bind us to the earth,
Spite of despondence, of the inhuman dearth
Of noble natures, of the gloomy days,
Of all the unhealthy and o'erdarkened ways
Made for our searching; yes, in spite of all,
Some shape of beauty moves away the pall
From our dark spirits.   Such the sun, the moon,
Trees old, and young, sprouting such a shady boon
For simple sheep; and such are daffodils
With the green world they live in; and clear rills
That for themselves a cooling covert make
'Gainst the hot season; the mid forest brake,
Rich with a sprinkling of fair musk-rose blooms:
And such too is the grandeur of the dooms
We have imagined for the mighty dead;
All lovely tales that we have heard or read:
An endless fountain of immortal drink,
Pouring unto us from the heaven's brink.

Nor do we merely feel these essences
For one short hour; no, even as the trees
That whisper round a temple become soon
Dear as the temple's self, so does the moon,
The passion poesy, glories infinite,
Haunt us till they become a cheering light
Unto our souls, and bound to us so fast,
That, whether there be shine, or gloom o'ercast,
They always must be with us, or we die.

John Keats.

[*Music*]

45

Psalm cl.

Praise ye the Lord.
Praise God in his sanctuary:
Praise him in the firmament of his power.
Praise him for his mighty acts:
Praise him according to his excellent greatness.
Praise him with the sound of the trumpet:
Praise him with the psaltery and harp.
Praise him with the timbrel and dance:
Praise him with stringed instruments and the pipe.
Praise him upon the loud cymbals:
Praise him upon the high sounding cymbals.
Let every thing that hath breath praise the Lord.
Praise ye the Lord.

PART FOUR

DOUBT

Producer:

Miss M. H. ALLEN.

Speakers:

ROBERT HARRIS

ION SWINLEY.

[*By kind permission of the Coliseum Management.*]

Music:

Selected by H. FOSTER CLARK.

" The Planets " (Holst), No. 5, Saturn (The Bringer of
    Old Age), Part I.   Columbia L1532R.

Symphony, No. 5 (Tchaikowsky), 2nd Movement.
                                        Columbia L2178.

Good Friday Music (Wagner's Parsifal).   H.M.V. DB. 1677.

" Tristan and Isolde " (Wagner), Prelude to Act 3.
                                        H.M.V. D1413.

Symphony, No. 5 (Tchaikowsky), 2nd Movement.
                                        Columbia L2179.

PROLOGUE

It is written in *The Pilgrim's Progress* that when Christian and Hopeful unlocked the dungeon door in Doubting Castle with the Key of Promise they came out into the King's Highway again. Once over the stile, that divided this from the dominion of Giant Despair, they erected a pillar on which they engraved the words, " Over the stile is the way to Doubting Castle which is kept by Giant Despair who despiseth the King of the Celestial Countrey and seeks to destroy his holy pilgrims." Alas! the sign has either fallen long since or is overgrown with moss. Not a pilgrim, however he may have rejoiced, but merrily hents that stile—only to find himself in the cold grey forecourt of the castle.

First there is the farewell to youth. The happy ease of friendship is suddenly shattered by the partings of life and dubiously the pilgrim looks out on the world that he must tread alone. His mind reaches out to the last parting of all and it is borne in upon him that the sorrow of loss is irreparable. Nature becomes the emblem of suffering. The seas are her Titanic tears. In the woods there is no comfort. We achieve neither truth nor rest. From hour to hour we ripe and ripe and then from hour to hour we rot and rot. We drop like the fruit of the tree, he thinks, even we, even so. Nor only is he himself thus deciduous but all greatness, all power must be made equal with the poor crooked scythe and spade, even Ozymandias, king of kings.

The dim and padded arms of fate draw him into a doubtful

quiet, and the icy shape of futility mocks him as he advances on his hopeless quest. He is swept with confused alarms in ignorant dark. There in desolation a voice, like the voice of Job is uplifted beating with empty echo against the Gate.

But now in darkness the pilgrim remembers the origin of hope. The aged eagle cannot stretch its wings, but prayer has wings when earthly pinions are spent. He is lost in the streets of the "City of Dreadful Night"—in the cold suburb of dead faith, dead hope, dead love. He has come to the end of the way. Very well, he will not faint. He sets the slughorn to his lips and undaunted plays the note of man's ultimate defiance. And in that moment there appears in the shadow of the dark Tower the Beloved Figure that has prevailed upon the dark. The pilgrim—doubting Thomas—lays his hands against the wounds, and becomes a symbol of hope to those blessed who have not seen and yet have believed.

Parting

O tell me, friends, while yet we part,
And heart can yet be heard of heart,
O tell me then, for what is it
Our early plan of life we quit;
From all our old intentions range,
And why does all so wholly change?
O tell me, friends, while yet we part!

O tell me, friends, while yet we hear,—
May it not be, some coming year,
These ancient paths that here divide
Shall yet again run side by side,
And you from there, and I from here,
All on a sudden reappear?
O tell me, friends, while yet ye hear!

O tell me, friends, ye hardly hear,—
And if indeed ye did, I fear
Ye would not say, ye would not speak,—
Are you so strong, am I so weak,
And yet, how much so e'er I yearn,
Can I not follow, nor you turn?
O tell me, friends, ye hardly hear!

O tell me, friends that are no more,
Do you, too, think ere it is o'er
Old times shall yet come round as erst,
And we be friends, as we were first?
Or do you judge that all is vain,
Except that rule that none complain?
O tell me, friends that are no more!

ARTHUR HUGH CLOUGH.

51

The End

After the blast of lightning from the east,
The flourish of loud clouds, the chariot throne,
After the drums of time have rolled and ceased
And from the bronze west long retreat is blown.

Shall life renew these bodies? Of a truth
All death will be anew, all tears assuage?
Or fill these void veins full again with youth
And wash with an immortal water age?

When I do ask white age, he saith not so,—
" My head hangs weighed with snow,"
And when I hearken to the Earth she saith
My fiery heart sinks aching. It is death.
Mine ancient scars shall not be glorified
Nor my titanic tears, the seas, be dried.

WILFRED OWEN.

Night and Morning Songs

I am tired of the wind—
O wind, wind, be quiet . . .
I am burdened by the days
Of waiting and long riot.
The heavy trees are thinned;
The clouds love their ways . . .
There's no rest in my mind.

When the wind falls the rain falls;
The air has no more breath.
The ceaseless " hush " of rain
Is what eternity saith.
The hills grow near and tall
Let down a misty mane . . .
Endlessness weighs on all.

GORDON BOTTOMLEY.

Dirge in the Woods

A wind sways the pines,
    And below
Not a breath of wild air;
Still as the mosses that glow
On the flooring and over the lines
Of the roots here and there.
The pine-tree drops its dead;
They are quiet, as under the sea.
Overhead, overhead,
Rushes life in a race,
As the clouds, the clouds chase;
    And we go,
And we drop like fruits of the tree,
      Even we,
      Even so.

GEORGE MEREDITH.

Ozymandias

I met a traveller from an antique land
  Who said: "Two vast and trunkless legs of stone
stand in the desert. Near them in the sand
  Half sunk, a shattered visage lies, whose frown
And wrinkled lip and sneer of cold command
Tell that its sculptor well those passions read
  Which yet survive, stamped in these lifeless things,
The hand that mocked them and the heart that fed.
And on the pedestal these words appear:
 'My name is Ozymandias, king of kings.
Look on my works, ye mighty, and despair!'
  Nothing beside remains. Round the decay
of that colossal wreck, boundless and bare,
  The lone and level sands stretch far away."

PERCY BYSSHE SHELLEY.

Futility

Sink, thou strange heart, unto thy rest.
Pine no more, to pine in vain.
Doth not the moon in heaven's breast
Call the floods home again?

Doth not the summer faint at last?
Do not her restless rivers flow
When that her transient day is past
To hide them in ice and snow?

All this—thy world—an end shall make;
Planet to sun return again;
The Universe, to sleep from wake,
In a last peace remain.

Alas, the futility of care
That, spinning thought to thought, doth weave
An idle argument in the air
We love not, nor believe.

WALTER DE LA MARE.

Dover Beach

The sea is calm to-night.
The tide is full, the moon lies fair
Upon the straits;—on the French coast the light
Gleams and is gone; the cliffs of England stand,
Glimmering and vast, out in the tranquil bay.
Come to the window, sweet is the night-air!
Only, from the long line of spray
Where the sea meets the moon-blanch'd land,
Listen! you hear the grating roar
Of pebbles which the waves draw back, and fling,

At their return, up the high strand,
Begin, and cease, and then again begin,
With tremulous cadence slow, and bring
The eternal note of sadness in.

Sophocles long ago
Heard it on the Aegean, and it brought
Into his mind the turbid ebb and flow
Of human misery ; we
Find also in the sound a thought,
Hearing it by this distant northern sea.

The Sea of Faith
Was once, too, at the full, and round earth's shore
Lay like the folds of a bright girdle furl'd.
But now I only hear
Its melancholy, long, withdrawing roar,
Retreating, to the breath
Of the night-wind, down the vast edges drear
And naked shingles of the world.

Ah, love, let us be true
To one another ! for the world, which seems
To lie before us like a land of dreams,
So various, so beautiful, so new,
Hath really neither joy, nor love, nor light,
Nor certitude, nor peace, nor help for pain ;
And we are here as on a darkling plain
Swept with confused alarms of struggle and flight,
Where ignorant armies clash by night.

MATTHEW ARNOLD.

Job xxiii. 1–10

Oh that I knew where I might find him,
That I might come even to his seat !
I would order my cause before him,
And fill my mouth with arguments.

I would know the words which he would answer me,
And understand what he would say unto me.
Would he contend with me in the greatness of his
    power?
Nay; but he would give heed unto me.
There the upright might reason with him;
So should I be delivered for ever from my judge.
Behold, I go forward, but he is not there;
And backward, but I cannot perceive him:
On the left hand, when he doth work, but I cannot
    behold him:
He hideth himself on the right hand, that I cannot see
    him.

Batter My Heart

Batter my heart, three-personed God! for you
As yet but knock; breathe, shine and seek to
    mend;
That I may rise, and stand, o'erthrow me, and
    bend
Your forces to break, blow, burn, and make me
    new.
I, like a usurped town, to another due,
Labour to admit you, but oh, to no end.
Reason, your viceroy in me, me should defend,
But is captured, and proves weak and untrue.
Yet dearly I love you, and would be loved fain,
But am betrothed unto your enemy;
Divorce me, untie, or break that knot again;
Take me to you, imprison me; for I,
Except you enthrall me, never shall be free.
Nor ever chaste, except you ravish me.

JOHN DONNE.

Extract from " The City of Dreadful Night "

Then turning to the right resumed his march,
  And travelled streets and lanes with wond'rous strength,
Until on stooping through a narrow arch
  We stood before a squalid house at length:
He gazed, and whispered with a cold despair,
Here Hope died, starved out in its utmost lair.

When he had spoken thus, before he stirred,
  I spoke, perplexed by something in the signs
Of desolation I had seen and heard
  In this drear pilgrimage to ruined shrines:
When Faith and Love and Hope are dead indeed,
Can Life still live? By what doth it proceed?

As whom his one intense thought overpowers,
  He answered coldly, Take a watch, erase
The signs and figures of the circling hours,
  Detach the hands, remove the dial-face;
The works proceed until run down; although
Bereft of purpose, void of use, still go.

Then turning to the right paced on again,
  And traversed squares and travelled streets whose glooms
Seemed more and more familiar to my ken;
  And reached that sullen temple of the tombs;
And paused to murmur with the old despair,
Here Faith died, poisoned by this charnel air.

I ceased to follow, for the knot of doubt
  Was severed sharply with a cruel knife:
He circled thus for ever tracing out
  The series of the fraction left of Life;
Perpetual recurrence in the scope
Of but three terms, dead Faith, dead Love, dead
  Hope.[1]   JAMES THOMSON (" B.V.").

[1] Life divided by that persistent three $= \dfrac{\text{LXX}}{333} = \cdot 2\dot{1}\dot{0}$.

57

From "Childe Roland"

Burningly it came on me all at once,
    This was the place! those two hills on the right,
    Crouched like two bulls locked horn in horn in fight;
While to the left, a tall scalped mountain . . . Dunce,
Fool, to be dozing at the very nonce,
    After a life spent training for the sight!

What in the midst lay but the Tower itself?
    The round squat turret, blind as the fool's heart,
    Built of brown stone, without a counterpart
In the whole world. The tempest's mocking elf
Points to the shipman thus the unseen shelf
    He strikes on, only when the timbers start.

Not see? because of night perhaps?—Why, day
    Came back again for that! before it left.
    The dying sunset kindled through a cleft:
The hills, like giants at a hunting, lay,
Chin upon hand, to see the game at bay,—
    "Now stab and end the creature—to the heft!"

Not hear? when noise was everywhere! it tolled
    Increasing like a bell. Names in my ears,
    Of all the lost adventurers my peers,—
How such a one was strong, and such was bold,
And such was fortunate, yet each of old
    Lost, lost! one moment knelled the woe of years.

There they stood, ranged along the hill-sides, met
    To view the last of me, a living frame
    For one more picture! in a sheet of flame
I saw them and I knew them all. And yet
Dauntless the slug-horn to my lips I set.
    And blew. "Childe Roland to the Dark Tower came."

                                        ROBERT BROWNING.

St. John xx. 19–31

When therefore it was evening, on that day, the first day of the week, and when the doors were shut where the disciples were, for fear of the Jews, Jesus came and stood in the midst, and saith unto them, Peace be unto you. And when he had said this, he shewed unto them his hands and his side. The disciples therefore were glad, when they saw the Lord. . . .

But Thomas, one of the twelve, called Didymus, was not with them when Jesus came. The other disciples therefore said unto him, We have seen the Lord. But he said unto them, Except I shall see in his hands the print of the nails, and put my finger into the print of the nails, and put my hand into his side, I will not believe.

And after eight days again his disciples were within, and Thomas with them. Jesus cometh, the doors being shut, and stood in the midst, and said, Peace be unto you. Then saith he to Thomas, Reach hither thy finger, and see my hands : and reach hither thy hand, and put it into my side : and be not faithless, but believing. Thomas answered and said unto him, My Lord and my God. Jesus saith unto him, Because thou hast seen me, thou hast believed : blessed are they that have not seen, and yet have believed.

PART FIVE

LOVE

Producer:

Miss M. H. ALLEN.

Speakers:

JANET TAYLOR.

ION SWINLEY.

ROBERT SPEAIGHT.

Music:

Selected by H. FOSTER CLARK.

Quartet in B Flat Major, No. 2 (Mozart), 1st Movement.
H.M.V. D1387.

Trio, No. 1, in B Flat, Op. 99 (Schubert), 2nd Movement.
H.M.V. DB949.

Quintet in A Major (Mozart), 2nd Movement.
Columbia 2253L.

Quintet in B Minor (Brahms), 1st and 2nd Movements.
Columbia 2229L.

Quintet in G Major (Brahms), 1st Movement.
H.M.V. DB1866.

Piano Quintet in F Minor (Brahms), Scherzo Allegro,
(*a*) Poco sostenuto, (*b*) Allegro non troppo.
Columbia L2043.

Quintet in B Minor (Brahms), 4th Movement.
Columbia L2232.

PROLOGUE

" THE greatest of these is Charity "—whose other and sweeter name is love. On the pilgrim's way this is the aeroplane moment, when the spirit leaves earth to mix with the wings and voices of the birds.

But even love has its phases—from the sickle moon to the last pale diamond, starring the forehead of encroaching night. There is youth's love, which calls to the beloved to share the overflowing sun. There is the exaltation of love, the praise of the beloved's excellence and her abounding grace. There is love's melancholy, when the whole world is blown like a single feather upon a sigh. There is then the farewell to the fair and lovely.

But the end of earthly love is the beginning of the love of heaven. That love does not change or lessen. It is patient, long-suffering, and in the end annihilates all else in its abiding radiance.

" Ah fondest, blindest, weakest,"
cries this Love to the Pilgrim,
" I am he who thou seekest,"
Thou dravest love from thee, who dravest Me.

From " *Corinna's Going a-Maying* "

Come, my Corinna, come; and coming, mark
How each field turns a street, each street a park,
   Made green and trimm'd with trees! see how
   Devotion gives each house a bough
   Or branch! each porch, each door, ere this,
   An ark, a tabernacle is,
Made up of white-thorn neatly interwove,
As if here were those cooler shades of love.
   Can such delights be in the street
   And open fields, and we not see't?
   Come, we'll abroad: and let's obey
   The proclamation made for May,
And sin no more, as we have done, by staying;
But, my Corinna, come, let's go a-Maying.

There's not a budding boy or girl this day
But is got up and gone to bring in May.
   A deal of youth ere this is come
   Back, and with white-thorn laden home.
   Some have despatch'd their cakes and cream,
   Before that we have left to dream:
And some have wept and woo'd, and plighted troth,
And chose their priest, ere we can cast off sloth:
   Many a green-gown has been given,
   Many a kiss, both odd and even:
   Many a glance, too, has been sent
   From out the eye, love's firmament:
Many a jest told of the keys betraying
This night, and locks pick'd: yet we're not a-Maying!

Come, let us go, while we are in our prime,
And take the harmless folly of the time!
   We shall grow old apace, and die
   Before we know our liberty.

Our life is short, and our days run
As fast away as does the sun.
And, as a vapour or a drop of rain,
Once lost, can ne'er be found again,
So when or you or I are made
A fable, song, or fleeting shade,
All love, all liking, all delight
Lies drown'd with us in endless night.
Then, while time serves, and we are but decaying,
Come, my Corinna, come, let's go a-Maying.

ROBERT HERRICK.

The Song of Solomon ii.

The voice of my beloved! behold, he cometh,
Leaping upon the mountains, skipping upon the hills.
My beloved is like a roe or a young hart:
Behold, he standeth behind our wall,
He looketh in at the windows,
He sheweth himself through the lattice.
My beloved spake, and said unto me,
Rise up, my love, my fair one, and come away.
For, lo, the winter is past,
The rain is over and gone;
The flowers appear on the earth;
The time of the singing of birds is come,
And the voice of the turtle is heard in our land;
The fig tree ripeneth her green figs,
And the vines are in blossom,
They give forth their fragrance.
Arise, my love, my fair one, and come away.
O my dove, that art in the clefts of the rock, in the
covert of the steep place,
Let me see thy countenance, let me hear thy voice;

For sweet is thy voice, and thy countenance is comely.
Take us the foxes, the little foxes, that spoil the
vineyards;
For our vineyards are in blossom.
My beloved is mine, and I am his:
He feedeth his flock among the lilies.
Until the day be cool, and the shadows flee away,
Turn, my beloved, and be thou like a roe or a young
hart
Upon the mountains of Bether.

The Song of Songs.

She Walks in Beauty

She walks in beauty, like the night
   Of cloudless climes and starry skies;
And all that's best of dark and bright
   Meet in her aspect and her eyes:
Thus mellow'd to that tender light
   Which heaven to gaudy day denies.

One shade the more, one ray the less,
   Had half impair'd the nameless grace
Which waves in every raven tress,
   Or softly lightens o'er her face;
Where thoughts serenely sweet express
   How pure, how dear their dwelling-place.

And on that cheek, and o'er that brow,
   So soft, so calm, yet eloquent,
The smiles that win, the tints that glow,
   But tell of days in goodness spent,
A mind at peace with all below,
   A heart whose love is innocent!

BYRON.

The Bargain

My true love hath my heart, and I have his,
  By just exchange one for another given:
I hold his dear, and mine he cannot miss,
  There never was a better bargain driven:
  My true love hath my heart, and I have his.

His heart in me keeps him and me in one,
  My heart in him his thoughts and senses guides:
He loves my heart, for once it was his own,
  I cherish his because in me it bides:
  My true love hath my heart, and I have his.

SIR PHILIP SIDNEY.

Go, Lovely Rose

Go, lovely Rose—
Tell her that wastes her time and me,
  That now she knows,
When I resemble her to thee,
How sweet and fair she seems to be.

Tell her that's young,
And shuns to have her graces spied,
  That hadst thou sprung
In deserts where no men abide,
Thou must have uncommended died.

Small is the worth
Of beauty from the light retired:
  Bid her come forth,
Suffer herself to be desired,
And not blush so to be admired.

Then die—that she
The common fate of all things rare
May read in thee;
How small a part of time they share
That are so wondrous sweet and fair!

EDMUND WALLER.

Summer Night

Now sleeps the crimson petal, now the white;
Nor waves the cypress in the palace walk;
Nor winks the gold fin in the porphyry font:
The firefly wakens: waken thou with me.

Now droops the milk-white peacock like a ghost,
And like a ghost she glimmers on to me.
Now lies the Earth all Danae to the stars,
And all thy heart lies open unto me.

Now slides the silent meteor on, and leaves
A shining furrow, as thy thoughts in me.

Now folds the lily all her sweetness up,
And slips into the bosom of the lake:
So fold thyself, my dearest, thou, and slip
Into my bosom and be lost in me.

TENNYSON.

Love's Deity

I long to talk with some old lover's ghost,
    Who died before the god of love was born.
I cannot think that he, who then loved most,
    Sunk so low as to love one which did scorn.

68

But since this god produced a destiny,
And that vice-nature, custom, lets it be,
 I must love her that loves not me.

Sure, they which made him god, meant not so much,
 Nor he in his young godhead practised it.
But when an even flame two hearts did touch,
 His office was indulgently to fit
Actives to passives. Correspondency
Only his subject was; it cannot be
 Love, till I love her, who loves me.

But every modern god will now extend
 His vast prerogative as far as Jove.
To rage, to lust, to write to, to commend,
 All is the purlieu of the god of love.
O! were we waken'd by this tyranny
To ungod this child again, it could not be
 I should love her, who loves not me.

Rebel and atheist too, why murmur I,
 As though I felt the worst that love could do?
Love might make me leave loving, or might try
 A deeper plague, to make her love me too:
Which, since she loves before, I'm loth to see.
Falsehood is worse than hate; and that must be,
 If she whom I love, should love me.

JOHN DONNE.

Departure

It was not like your great and gracious ways!
Do you, that have naught other to lament,
Never, my Love, repent
Of how, that July afternoon,
You went,
With sudden, unintelligible phrase,
And frighten'd eye,

Upon your journey of so many days
Without a single kiss, or a good-bye?
I knew, indeed, that you were parting soon;
And so we sate, within the low sun's rays,
You whispering to me, for your voice was weak,
Your harrowing praise.
Well, it was well
To hear you such things speak,
And I could tell
What made your eyes a growing gloom of love,
As a warm South-wind sombres a March grove.
And it was like your great and gracious ways
To turn your talk on daily things, my Dear,
Lifting the luminous, pathetic lash
To let the laughter flash,
Whilst I drew near,
Because you spoke so low that I could scarcely hear.
But all at once to leave me at the last,
More at the wonder than the loss aghast,
With huddled, unintelligible phrase,
And frighten'd eye,
And go your journey of all days
With not one kiss, or a good-bye,
And the only loveless look the look with which you
    pass'd:
'Twas all unlike your great and gracious ways.

COVENTRY PATMORE.

Music, when Soft Voices Die

Music, when soft voices die,
Vibrates in the memory;
Odours, when sweet violets sicken,
Live within the sense they quicken.

70

Rose leaves, when the rose is dead,
Are heap'd for the belovèd's bed;
And so thy thoughts, when thou art gone,
Love itself shall slumber on.

PERCY BYSSHE SHELLEY.

Fidele

Fear no more the heat o' the sun,
  Nor the furious winter's rages;
Thou thy worldly task hast done,
  Home art gone, and ta'en thy wages:
Golden lads and girls all must,
As chimney-sweepers, come to dust.

Fear no more the frown o' the great,
  Thou art past the tyrant's stroke;
Care no more to clothe and eat;
  To thee the reed is as the oak:
The sceptre, learning, physic, must
All follow this, and come to dust.

Fear no more the lightning-flash,
  Nor the all-dreaded thunder-stone;
Fear not slander, censure rash;
  Thou hast finish'd joy and moan:
All lovers young, all lovers must
Consign to thee, and come to dust.

No exorciser harm thee!
Nor no witchcraft charm thee!
Ghost unlaid forbear thee!
Nothing ill come near thee!
Quiet consummation have;
And renowned be thy grave!

WILLIAM SHAKESPEARE.

71

From " Exequy on his Wife "

Sleep on, my Love, in thy cold bed
Never to be disquieted!
My last good night! Thou wilt not wake
Till I thy fate shall overtake:
Till age, or grief, or sickness must
Marry my body to that dust
It so much loves; and fill the room
My heart keeps empty in thy tomb.
Stay for me there: I will not fail
To meet thee in that hollow vale.
And think not much of my delay:
I am already on the way,
And follow thee with all the speed
Desire can make, or sorrows breed.
Each minute is a short degree
And every hour a step towards thee. . . .
'Tis true—with shame and grief I yield—
Thou, like the van, first took'st the field;
And gotten hast the victory
In thus adventuring to die
Before me, whose more years might crave
A just precedence in the grave.
But hark! my pulse, like a soft drum,
Beats my approach, tells thee I come;
And slow howe'er my marches be
I shall at last sit down by thee.
The thought of this bids me go on
And wait my dissolution
With hope and comfort. Dear—forgive
The crime—I am content to live
Divided, with but half a heart,
Till we shall meet and never part.

HENRY KING.

72

Love

Love bade me welcome; yet my soul drew back,
    Guilty of dust and sin.
But quick-eyed Love, observing me grow slack
    From my first entrance in,
Drew nearer to me, sweetly questioning
    If I lack'd anything.

" A guest," I answer'd, " worthy to be here ":
    Love said, " You shall be he."
" I, the unkind, ungrateful? Ah, my dead,
    I cannot look on Thee."
Love took my hand and smiling did reply,
    " Who made the eyes but I? "

" Truth, Lord; but I have marr'd them: let my shame
    Go where it doth deserve."
" And know you not," says Love, " Who bore the blame?"
    " My dear, then I will serve."
" You must sit down," says Love, " and taste my meat."
    So I did sit and eat.

                 GEORGE HERBERT.

From " The Hound of Heaven "

That Voice is round me like a bursting sea:
    " And is thy earth so marred
    Shattered in shard on shard?
Lo, all things fly thee, for thou fliest Me!
Strange, piteous, futile thing!
Wherefore should any set thee love apart?
Seeing none but I makes much of naught " (He said),
" And human love needs human meriting:
    How hast thou merited—

Of all man's clotted clay the dingiest clot?
　　Alack, thou knowest not
How little worthy of any love thou art!
Whom wilt thou find to love ignoble thee,
　　Save Me, save only Me?
All which I took from thee I did but take,
　　Not for thy harms
But just that thou might'st seek it in My arms.
　　All which thy child's mistake
Fancies as lost, I have stored for thee at home:
　　Rise, clasp my hand, and come!"

　　　Halts by me that footfall:
　　　Is my gloom, after all,
　Shade of His hand, outstretched caressingly?
　　　" Ah, fondest, blindest, weakest,
　　　I am He whom thou seekest."
　Thou dravest love from thee, who dravest Me.

FRANCIS THOMPSON

PART SIX

CONTEMPLATION

Producer :
Miss M. H. ALLEN.

Speakers :
ROBERT HARRIS.
[*By kind permission of St. Martin's Theatre Management.*]
ION SWINLEY.
[*By kind permission of the Coliseum Management.*]

Music :
Selected by H. FOSTER CLARK.

Choral Prelude (Bach).   H.M.V. DB1789.

Symphony, No. 1, in A Flat Major (Elgar), 4th Movement.   H.M.V. D1948.

Saint Sebastian (Debussy).   H.M.V. DB4817.

Orpheus—Dance of the Blessed Spirits (Gluck).   H.M.V. D1784.

Shepherds' Christmas Dance (Bach).   H.M.V. D1741.

PROLOGUE

THERE is a pause on the way while the pilgrim, laying aside scrip and pack, sits by the roadside thinking upon the past, the present and the future. This is the hour of the inward eye—which is the bliss of solitude. Contemplation takes one soft step and stands at the pilgrim's side.

The pilgrim may occupy himself with the significance immediately under his eyes—the small bright movements of life as it passes. Or he may seek to find the deeper truth behind incessant memory, finding the everlasting in the instant. Or he may cast back to the freshness of youth for ever lost, or console himself by the assurance that it has become a constant in his heart. He may remember the groves of Eden and find himself still a countryman walking there by right.

If he look forward he may glimpse the cold face of death, and wonder, as he shrinks back, whether he will meet him before he has reached the delectable Mountains. But, if he sink deep enough, he will realize that the way is not measured by miles. One step in the sun's eye and he may be reborn into the first dream. And as he rises to his feet to resume the long travail he may be aware of a sudden comfort. He has been made to lie down in green pastures. The Shepherd is at hand.

Leisure

What is this life if, full of care,
We have no time to stand and stare.

No time to stand beneath the boughs
And stare as long as sheep or cows.

No time to see, when woods we pass,
Where squirrels hide their nuts in grass.

No time to see, in broad daylight,
Streams full of stars, like skies at night.

No time to turn at Beauty's glance,
And watch her feet, how they can dance.

No time to wait till her mouth can
Enrich that smile her eyes began.

A poor life this if, full of care,
We have no time to stand and stare.

W. H. DAVIES.

Mark xii.

All we have is God's, and yet
Cæsar challenges a debt;
Nor hath God a thinner share
Whatever Cæsar's payments are.

All is God's; and yet, 'tis true,
All we have is Cæsar's too.
All is Cæsar's; and what odds
So long as Cæsar's self is God's?

RICHARD CRASHAW.

78

Auguries of Innocence

To see a World in a grain of sand,
And a Heaven in a wild flower,
Hold Infinity in the palm of your hand,
And Eternity in an hour. . . .

The bat that flits at close of eve
Has left the brain that won't believe.
The owl that calls upon the night
Speaks the unbeliever's fright. . . .

Joy and woe are woven fine,
A clothing for the soul divine;
Under every grief and pine
Runs a joy with silken twine. . . .

Every tear from every eye
Becomes a babe in Eternity. . . .

The bleat, the bark, bellow, and roar
Are waves that beat on Heaven's shore. . . .

He who doubts from what he sees
Will ne'er believe, do what you please.
If the Sun and Moon should doubt,
They'd immediately go out. . . .

God appears, and God is Light,
To those poor souls who dwell in Night;
But does a human form display
To those who dwell in realms of Day.

WILLIAM BLAKE.

From " The Scholar-Gipsy "

O born in days when wits were fresh and clear,
    And life ran gaily as the sparkling Thames;
        Before this strange disease of modern life,
With its sick hurry, its divided aims,
    It's heads o'ertax'd, its palsied hearts, was rife—
        Fly hence, our contact fear!
Still fly, plunge deeper in the bowering wood!
    Averse, as Dido did with gesture stern
    From her false friend's approach in Hades turn,
Wave us away, and keep thy solitude!

Still nursing the unconquerable hope,
    Still clutching the inviolable shade,
        With a free, onward impulse brushing through,
By night, the silver'd branches of the glade—
    Far on the forest-skirts, where none pursue,
        On some mild pastoral slope
Emerge, and resting on the moonlit pales
    Freshen thy flowers as in former years
    With dew, or listen with enchanted ears,
From the dark dingles, to the nightingales!

                                    MATTHEW ARNOLD.

From " Lines Composed a few Miles above Tintern Abbey "

For I have learned
To look on nature, not as in the hour
Of thoughtless youth; but hearing oftentimes
The still, sad music of humanity,
Nor harsh nor grating, though of ample power

80

To chasten and subdue.   And I have felt
A presence that disturbs me with the joy
Of elevated thoughts; a sense sublime
Of something far more deeply interfused,
Whose dwelling is the light of setting suns,
And the round ocean and the living air,
And the blue sky, and in the mind of man:
A motion and a spirit, that impels
All thinking things, all objects of all thought,
And rolls through all things.   Therefore am I still
A lover of the meadows and the woods,
And mountains; and of all that we behold
From this green earth; of all the mighty world
Of eye, and ear—both what they half create,
And what perceive; well pleased to recognise
In nature and the language of the sense,
The anchor of my purest thoughts, the nurse,
The guide, the guardian of my heart, and soul
Of all my moral being.

WILLIAM WORDSWORTH.

Montserrat

Peace waits among the hills;
I have drunk peace,
Here, where the blue air fills
The great cup of the hills,
And fills with peace.

Between the earth and sky,
I have seen the earth
Like a dark cloud go by,
And fade out of the sky;
There was no more earth.

Here, where the Holy Graal
Brought secret light
Once, from beyond the veil,
I, seeing no Holy Graal,
See divine light.

Light fills the hills with God,
Wind with his breath,
And here, in his abode,
Light, wind, and air praise God,
And this poor breath.

ARTHUR SYMONS.

From " Il Penseroso "

Oft on a plat of rising ground,
I hear the far-off Curfeu sound,
Over some wide-water's shoar,
Swinging slow with sullen roar;
Or if the Ayr will not permit,
Som still removed place will fit,
Where glowing Embers through the room
Teach light to counterfeit a gloom,
Far from all resort of mirth,
Save the Cricket on the hearth,
Or the Belman's drousie charm,
To bless the dores from nightly harm:
Or let my Lamp at midnight hour
Be seen in som high lonely Towr,
Where I may oft outwatch the Bear,
With thrice great Hermes, or unsphear
The spirit of Plato to unfold
What Worlds, or what vast Regions hold
The immortal mind that hath forsook
Her mansion in this fleshly nook:

82

And of those Daemons that are found
In fire, air, flood, or under ground,
Whose power hath a true consent
With Planet, or with Element.

JOHN MILTON.

Sonnet Written in January 1818

When I have fears that I may cease to be
Before my pen has gleaned my teeming brain,
Before high-piled books, in charact'ry,
Hold like full garners the full-ripened grain;
When I behold, upon the night's starred face,
Huge cloudy symbols of a high romance,
And feel that I may never live to trace
Their shadows, with the magic hand of chance;
And when I feel, fair creature of an hour!
That I shall never look upon thee more,
Never have relish in the faery power
Of unreflecting love!—then on the shore
Of the wide world I stand alone, and think
Till Love and Fame to nothingness do sink.

JOHN KEATS.

The Garden

Meanwhile the mind, from pleasure less,
Withdraws into its happiness;
The mind, that ocean where each kind
Does straight its own resemblance find;
Yet it creates, transcending these,
Far other worlds and other seas,
Annihilating all that's made
To a green thought in a green shade.

83

Here at the fountain's sliding foot
Or at some fruit tree's mossy root,
Casting the body's vest aside
My soul into the boughs does glide:
There, like a bird, it sits and sings,
Then whets and claps its silver wings,
And, till prepared for longer flight,
Waves in its plumes the various light. . . .

Such was the happy Garden-state
While man there walked without a mate:
After a place so pure and sweet,
What other help could yet be meet!
But 'twas beyond a mortal's share
To wander solitary there:
Two paradises 'twere in one,
To live in Paradise alone. . . .

ANDREW MARVELL.

To a Daisy

Slight as thou art, thou art enough to hide,
　Like all created things, secrets from me,
　And stand a barrier to eternity.
And I, how can I praise thee well and wide.

From where I dwell—upon the hither side?
　Thou little veil for so great mystery,
　When shall I penetrate all things and thee
And then look back? For this I must abide.

Till thou shalt grow and fold and be unfurled
Literally between me and the world.
　Then shall I drink from in beneath a spring,

And from a poet's side shall read his book.
O daisy mine, what will it be to look
   From God's side even of such a simple thing?

ALICE MEYNELL.

Sonnet composed upon Westminster Bridge,
3rd September 1802

Earth has not anything to show more fair:
Dull would he be of soul who could pass by
A sight so touching in its majesty:
This City now doth, like a garment, wear
The beauty of the morning; silent, bare,
Ships, towers, domes, theatres, and temples lie
Open unto the fields, and to the sky;
All bright and glittering in the smokeless air.
Never did sun more beautifully steep
In his first splendour, valley, rock, or hill;
Ne'er saw I, never felt, a calm so deep!
The river glideth at his own sweet will:
Dear God! the very houses seem asleep;
And all that mighty heart is lying still!

WILLIAM WORDSWORTH.

The Busy Heart

Now that we've done our best and worst, and parted,
   I would fill my mind with thoughts that will not rend.
(O heart, I do not dare go empty-hearted)
   I'll think of Love in books, Love without end;
Women with child, content; and old men sleeping;
   And wet strong ploughlands, scarred for certain grain;
And babes that weep, and so forget their weeping;
   And the young heavens, forgetful after rain;

85

And evening hush, broken by homing wings;
   And Song's nobility, and Wisdom holy,
That live, we dead. I would think of a thousand things,
   Lovely and durable, and taste them slowly,
One after one, like tasting a sweet food.
I have need to busy my heart with quietude.

RUPERT BROOKE.

The Seeker

I sat me down and looked around
The little lamp-lit room, and saw
Where many pictures gloomed and frowned
In sad, still life, nor made a sound—
A many for one to draw:
    Shadow and sea and ground
    Held by the artist's law,
    Beauty without a flaw,
    All with a sense profound.

One teeming brain was wood and hill,
And sloping pastures wide and green,
And cool deep seas where rivers spill
The snows of mountains far and chill,
Sad pools where the shadows lean.
    Old trees that hang so still.
    Fields which the reapers glean.
    Plains where the wind is keen.
    Each with a nerve to thrill.

Elusive figures swayed and yearned
By lake and misty greenwood dim,
Seeking in sorrow: they had learned
In one night's dream might be discerned,
A pace from the world's rim,

Wages their woe had earned,
Rest from the labour grim,
God and the peace of Him—
These in a frame interned.

.   .   .   .   .

On through the forest, one step on,
One step, O Powers, let me attain
This hard, dead step, let me begone,
Back where I and the morning shone,
Back ere the dream shall wane
    When I and a star were one.
    Seen through the veils of pain
    Glory shall shine again :
    God, has the vision gone?

JAMES STEPHENS.

From " The Psalms "

viii. 3, 4

FIRST VOICE: I will consider thy heavens, even the works of thy fingers : the moon and the stars, which thou hast ordained.

What is man, that thou art mindful of him; and the son of man, that thou visitest him?

lxiii. 7, 8

SECOND VOICE: Have I not remembered thee in my bed : and thought upon thee when I was waking?

Because thou hast been my helper; therefore under the shadow of thy wings will I rejoice.

lxxvii. 5–12

FIRST VOICE: I have considered the days of old: and the years that are passed.

I call to remembrance my song: and in the night I commune with mine own heart, and search out my spirits.

Will the Lord absent himself for ever: and will he be no more intreated?

Is his mercy clean gone for ever: and is his promise come utterly to an end for evermore?

Hath God forgotten to be gracious: and will he shut up his loving-kindness in displeasure?

And I said, it is mine own infirmity: but I will remember the years of the right hand of the most Highest.

I will remember the works of the Lord: and call to mind thy wonders of old time.

I will think also of all thy works.

The Scribe

What lovely things
  Thy hand hath made:
The smooth-plumed bird
  In its emerald shade,
The seed of the grass,
  The speck of stone
Which the wayfaring ant
  Stirs—and hastes on!

Though I should sit
  By some tarn in thy hills,
Using its ink
  As the spirit wills

To write of earth's wonders,
   Its live, willed things,
Flit would the ages
   On soundless wings
Ere unto Z
   My pen drew nigh;
Leviathan told,
   And the honey-fly:

And still would remain
   My wit to try—
My worn reeds broken,
   The dark tarn dry,
All words forgotten—
   Thou, Lord, and I.

WALTER DE LA MARE.

PART SEVEN

FEAR

Producer:
Miss M. H. ALLEN.

Speakers:
ROBERT SPEAIGHT.
ION SWINLEY.

Music:
Selected by H. FOSTER CLARK.

Apollon Musagetes Ballet (Stravinsky). H.M.V. D2096.
Death and Transfiguration, Op. 24 (Strauss).
                                    H.M.V. D1525.
Symphonic Fantasia, " Pohjola's Daughter " (Sibelius).
                                    H.M.V. DB1743.

PROLOGUE

THERE is fear waiting for every adventurer: all pilgrimage is an adventure, and fear must be overcome, if man is to tread happily the Pilgrim's Way. Born to suffer fear, man chooses also to inflict it, whether as discipline or punishment. In childhood fear gives a tang to experiences which to the adult are dulled by familiarity. Grown men and women will recover the sharpness of those childish fears when they are suddenly made aware of the fear which they inflict on animals, or themselves come into abrupt contact with the penalties of crime: and for some there is always the fear of the supernatural; fear which springs from the uneasy suspicion that there is something on the other side of a door, or in the dark places of the night, something beyond the reckoning of reason, something they can neither anticipate nor control.

" Men fear death as children fear to go into the dark " . . . that saying of the philosopher has great truth in it. All fear is the fear of death—of a thing not known to us by experience, for are we not alive?—but the presence of it in our midst, and the rumour of it in human history threaten our desires and enfeeble our energies. Fear of the unknown is ultimately a symbol of the fear of death, which is, for the natural man, a fear that he cannot conquer by his own strength.

Yet that fear has been conquered. From the beginning man has fought against it, devoting himself to works which would have no meaning, did death end all. Natural fear, the fear which shackles and enslaves us, can be banished by the fear of God, that beginning of wisdom which is refreshment and the strength to the pilgrim. In that reverend fear the lesser fears, which are its shadow, vanish and lose their authority; that fear alone can enhearten a man so that he will overcome the fear of death. There is no ignominy in the fear of God, and no shame. The pilgrim who entertains it faithfully will find all his difficulties at an end. He can go forward in the certainty of victory over fear, over himself and over the world.

North-West Passage

1. GOOD NIGHT

When the bright lamp is carried in,
The sunless hours again begin;
O'er all without, in field and lane,
The haunted night returns again.

Now we behold the embers flee
About the firelit hearth; and see
Our faces painted as we pass,
Like pictures, on the window-glass.

Must we to bed indeed? Well then,
Let us arise and go like men,
And face with an undaunted tread
The long black passage up to bed.

Farewell, O brother, sister, sire!
O pleasant party round the fire!
The songs you sing, the tales you tell,
Till far tomorrow, fare ye well!

2. SHADOW MARCH

All round the house is the jet-black night;
    It stares through the window-pane;
It crawls in the corners, hiding from the light,
    It moves with the moving flame.

Now my little heart goes a-beating like a drum,
    With the breath of the Bogie in my hair;
And all round the candle the crooked shadows come
    And go marching along up the stair.

95

The shadow of the balusters, the shadow of the lamp,
  The shadow of the child that goes to bed—
All the wicked shadows coming, tramp, tramp, tramp,
  With the black night overhead.

ROBERT LOUIS STEVENSON.

From " The Haunted and the Haunters "

Three slow, loud, distinct knocks were now heard at the bed-head; my servant called out, " Is that you, sir? "

" No; be on your guard."

The dog now roused himself and sat on his haunches, his ears moving quickly backwards and forwards. He kept his eyes fixed on me with a look so strange that he concentrated all my attention on himself. Slowly he rose up, all his hair bristling, and stood perfectly rigid, and with the same wild stare. I had no time, however, to examine the dog. Presently my servant emerged from his room; and if ever I saw horror in the human face, it was then. I should not have recognised him had we met in the streets, so altered was every lineament. He passed by me quickly, saying in a whisper that seemed scarcely to come from his lips, " Run—run! it is after me! " He gained the door to the landing, pulled it open and rushed forth. I followed him into the landing involuntarily, calling him to stop; but, without heeding me, he bounded down the stairs, clinging to the balusters, and taking several steps at a time. I heard, where I stood, the street-door open—heard it again clap to. I was left alone in the haunted house. . . .

I returned to my room, shut and locked the door that opened upon the interior one, and stood on the hearth, expectant and prepared. I now perceived that the dog had slunk into an angle of the wall, and was pressing himself close against it, as if literally trying to force his way into it. I approached the animal and spoke to it; the poor brute was evidently beside itself with terror. It showed all its teeth, the slaver dropping from its jaws, and would certainly have bitten me if I had touched it. It did not seem to recognise me. Whoever has seen at the Zoological Gardens a rabbit fascinated by a serpent, cowering in a corner, may form some idea of the anguish which the dog exhibited.

I strove to speak—my voice utterly failed me; I could only think to myself, " Is this fear? It is *not* fear! " I strove to rise—in vain; I felt as if weighed down by an irresistible force. Indeed, my impression was that of an immense and overwhelming Power opposed to my volition; that sense of utter inadequacy to cope with a force beyond men's, which one may feel *physically* in a storm at sea, in a conflagration, or when confronting some terrible wild beast, or rather, perhaps, the shark of the ocean, I felt *morally*. Opposed to my will was another will, as far superior to its strength as storm, fire, and shark are superior in material force to the force of men.

And now, as this impression grew on me, now came, at last, horror—horror to a degree that no words can convey. Still I retained pride, if not courage; and in my own mind I said: " This is horror, but it is not fear; unless I fear, I cannot be harmed; my reason rejects this thing; it is an illusion—I do not fear."

BULWER-LYTTON.

The Snare

I hear a sudden cry of pain !
There is a rabbit in a snare :
Now I hear the cry again,
But I cannot tell from where.

But I cannot tell from where
He is calling out for aid ;
Crying on the frightened air,
Making everything afraid.

Making everything afraid,
Wrinkling up his little face,
As he cries again for aid;
And I cannot find the place!

And I cannot find the place
Where his paw is in the snare:
Little one! Oh, little one!
I am searching everywhere.

JAMES STEPHENS.

From " The Ballad of Reading Gaol "

That night the empty corridors
   Were full of forms of Fear,
And up and down the iron town
   Stole feet we could not hear,
And through the bars that hide the stars
   White faces seemed to peer.

He lay as one who lies and dreams
   In a pleasant meadow-land,
The watchers watched him as he slept,
   And could not understand
How one could sleep so sweet a sleep
   With a hangman close at hand.

But there is no sleep when men must weep
   Who never yet have wept:
So we—the fool, the fraud; the knave—
   That endless vigil kept,
And through each brain on hands of pain
   Another's terror crept.

Alas! it is a fearful thing
  To feel another's guilt!
For, right within, the sword of Sin
  Pierced to its poisoned hilt,
And as molten lead were the tears we shed
  For the blood we had not spilt.

The Warders with their shoes of felt
  Crept by each padlocked door,
And peeped and saw, with eyes of awe,
  Grey figures on the floor,
And wondered why men knelt to pray
  Who never prayed before.

All through the night we knelt and prayed,
  Mad mourners of a corse!
The troubled plumes of midnight were
  The plumes upon a hearse:
And bitter wine upon a sponge
  Was the savour of Remorse.

OSCAR WILDE.

From " On Life," xxvii.

Men who have not understood life cannot help being
afraid of death. They see it and believe in it.

" No death? " these men indignantly and angrily exclaim.
" That is a sophistry. Death is before our eyes, it has mown
down millions and will mow us down too. However much
you may say that it does not exist, it is with us all the time.
. . . Look at it! "

And they do indeed see what they speak of—as a man
who is mentally deranged sees the ghost that frightens him:
He cannot touch that ghost, which has never touched him;

he knows nothing of its intentions, but this imaginary ghost causes him so much fear and suffering that he is deprived of capacity to live. And it is the same with death. Man does not know his own death and can never know it: it has never yet touched him and he knows nothing of its intentions. Of what, then, is he afraid?

LEO TOLSTOY.

In Plague Time

Adieu, farewell earth's bliss,
This world uncertain is;
Fond are life's lustful joys,
Death proves them all but toys,
None from his darts can fly.
I am sick, I must die.
    Lord, have mercy on us!

Rich men, trust not in wealth,
Gold cannot buy you health;
Physic himself must fade,
All things to end are made.
The plague full swift goes by.
I am sick, I must die.
    Lord, have mercy on us!

Beauty is but a flower
Which wrinkles will devour;
Brightness falls from the air,
Queens have died young and fair,
Dust hath closed Helen's eye.
I am sick, I must die.
    Lord, have mercy on us!

Strength stoops unto the grave,
Worms feed on Hector brave,
Swords may not fight with fate,
Earth still holds ope her gate.
Come! come! the bells do cry.
I am sick, I must die.
    Lord, have mercy on us!

Wit with his wantonness
Tasteth death's bitterness;
Hell's executioner
Hath no ears for to hear
What vain art can reply.
I am sick, I must die.
    Lord, have mercy on us!

Haste, therefore, each degree,
To welcome destiny,
Heaven is our heritage,
Earth but a player's stage;
Mount we unto the sky.
I am sick, I must die.
    Lord, have mercy on us!

                    THOMAS NASHE.

From " Lavengro," Ch. xviii.

O, the dark feeling of mysterious dread which comes over
the mind, and which the lamp of reason, though burning
bright the while, is unable to dispel! Art thou, as leeches
say, the concomitant of disease? ... Nay, rather the principle of woe itself, the fountain head of all sorrow co-existent
with man, whose influence he feels when yet unborn, for
... woe doth he bring with him into the world, even thy-

self, dark one, terrible one, causeless, unbegotten, without a father. . . . Then is it not lawful for man to exclaim, " Better that I had never been born ! " Fool, for thyself thou wast not born, but to fulfil the inscrutable decrees of thy Creator; and how dost thou know that this dark principle is not . . . thy best friend; that it is not that which tempers the whole mass of thy corruption? It may be, for what thou knowest, the mother of wisdom, and of great works: it is the dread of the horror of the night that makes the pilgrim hasten on his way. When thou feelest it nigh, let thy safety word be " Onward "; if thou tarry, thou art overwhelmed. Courage ! build great works—'tis urging thee—it is ever nearest the favourites of God—the fool knows little of it. Thou wouldst be joyous, wouldst thou? then be a fool. What great work was ever the result of joy, the puny one? Who have been the wise ones, the mighty ones, the conquering ones of this earth? the joyous? I believe (it) not.

GEORGE BORROW.

Psalm lv. 1–8

Give ear to my prayer, O God; and hide not thyself from my supplication.

Attend unto me, and answer me; I am restless in my complaint, and moan.

Because of the voice of the enemy, because of the oppression of the wicked; for they cast iniquity upon me, and in anger they persecute me.

My heart is sore pained within me; and the terrors of death are fallen upon me.

Fearfulness and trembling are come upon me, and horror hath overwhelmed me.

And I said, Oh that I had wings like a dove! then would I fly away, and be at rest.

Lo, then would I wander far off, I would lodge in the wilderness.

I would haste me to a shelter from the stormy wind and tempest.

To Christ

Wilt thou forgive that sinn, where I begunn,
  Which is my sinn, though it were done before?
Wilt thou forgive those sinns through which I runn
  And doe them still, though still I doe deplore?
    When thou hast done, thou hast not done,
      for I have more.

Wilt thou forgive that sinn, by which I'have wonne
  Others to sinn, & made my sinn their dore?
Wilt thou forgive that sinn which I did shunne
  A yeare or twoe, but wallowed in a score?
    When thou hast done, thou hast not done,
      for I have more.

I have a sinn of feare that when I have spunn
  My last thred, I shall perish on the shore;
Sweare by thy self that at my Death, thy Sunn
  Shall shine as it shines nowe, & heretofore;
    And having done that, thou hast done,
      I have noe more.

JOHN DONNE.

From " Last Fruit off an Old Tree "

Death stands above me, whispering low
I know not what into my ear:
Of his strange language all I know
Is, there is not a word of fear.

WALTER SAVAGE LANDOR.

From " Revelations of Divine Love," Ch. lxxiv.

Love and Dread are brethren, and they are rooted in us by the Goodness of our Maker, and they shall never be taken from us without end. We have of nature to love and we have of grace to love: and we have of nature to dread, and we have of grace to dread. It belongeth to the Lordship and to the Fatherhood to be dreaded, as it belongeth to the Goodness to be loved: and it belongeth to us that are His servants and His children to dread Him for Lordship and Fatherhood, as it belongeth to love Him for Goodness.

And though this reverent-dread and love be not parted asunder, yet they are not both one, but they are two in property and in working, and neither of them may be had without other. Therefore I am sure, he that loveth, he dreadeth, though that he feel it but a little.

JULIAN OF NORWICH.

The First Epistle of St. John, iv. 18

There is no fear in love: but perfect love casteth out fear, because fear hath punishment; and he that feareth is not made perfect in love.

PART EIGHT

COURAGE

Producer:

Miss M. H. ALLEN.

Speakers:

ION SWINLEY.

DENNIS ARUNDELL.

[*By kind permission of Horace Watson.*]

Music:

Selected by H. FOSTER CLARK.

Nocturne 2—Fêtes (Debussy). H.M.V. E 507.

" Parsifal " (Wagner), Prelude. H.M.V. D1025.

Symphonic Study, " Falstaff," Op. 68 (Elgar).
H.M.V. DB1624.

Fanfares by the Kneller Hall Musicians. H.M.V. C2445.

PROLOGUE

COURAGE is a bell in the dark. It rings when there is none by to help and before the sun is up. It can be heard far, like the trumpets of a relieving army. Its essence is of the soul, and like that its strength and its victory are not in the body's despite but in bending it to the higher purpose. It ranges from the desperate act of extreme fear to the great calm in which the grave has lost its victory and death has no sting.

The pilgrim being, therefore, of good heart, will ask of life full measure. He will not seek the quiet by-paths or be content with difficulty avoided. Not without sweat and heat are the crowns to be gained, and he will gladly tread where the throng is hottest. He will not merely not refuse, he will demand, the forlorn hope. For courage is then brightest when its reward is least apparent or expected. His heart is highest who, when all the world has failed honour and him, unsummoned by aught but his own spirit sets out on the last impossible Crusade.

The courage of the warrior is active sacrifice of all the lesser for the greater things, to throw life like a pearl into the styes of death knowing that in the end it will be found again. But the choice of courage is bitter because it is not given to many to know which are the lesser and which the greater things. This active courage therefore is a wisdom of the soul. As is no less that passive courage of endurance which life not seldom asks of women. It is a commonplace to exalt this courage over the other, but women, who know both, and are capable of both, would not have it so. Each is a bright weapon in the armoury of God.

Here are two weapons in the shape of a Cross which hangs above the world, the sign and symbol of courage that is both active in the conquest of evil and passive in its endurance of death's temporal offensive. Against this virtue death beats in vain like a black tide at the foot of an immutable cliff. The waters moan, rage and fall back in sullen defeat. The cliff is not shaken, altered or perturbed.

Credo

Away with funeral music, set
   The pipe to powerful lips—
The cup of life's for him that drinks
   And not for him that sips.

               ROBERT LOUIS STEVENSON.

Prayer

God, though this life is but a wraith
   Although we know not what we use,
Although we grope with little faith
   Give me the heart to fight—and lose.

Ever insurgent let me be,
   Make me more daring than devout;
From slack contentment keep me free,
   And fill me with a buoyant doubt.

Open my ears to visions girt
   With beauty and with wonder lit—
But let me always see the dirt
   And all that spawn and die in it.

Open my eyes to music; let
   Me thrill with spring's first flutes and drums—
But never let me dare forget
   The bitter ballads of the slums.

From compromise and things half done,
   Keep me, with stern and stubborn pride,
And when, at last, the fight is won
   God keep me still unsatisfied.

               LOUIS UNTERMEYER.

Henry V

WEST: O that we now had here
But one ten thousand of those men in England
That do no work to-day!

KING HENRY: What's he that wishes so?
My cousin Westmoreland? No, my fair cousin;
If we are marked to die, we enow
To do our country loss; and if to live,
The fewer men, the greater share of honour.
God's will! I pray thee, wish not one man more.
By Jove, I am not covetous for gold,
Nor care I who doth feed upon my cost;
It yearns me not if men my garments wear;
Such outward things dwell not in my desires:
But if it be a sin to covet honour,
I am the most offending soul alive.
No, faith, my coz, wish not a man from England:
God's peace! I would not lose so great an honour
As one man more, methinks, would share from me,
For the best hope I have. O, do not wish one
        more!
Rather proclaim it, Westmoreland, through my host,
That he which hath no stomach to his fight,
Let him depart; his passport shall be made
And crowns for convoy put into his purse:
We would not die in that man's company
That fears his fellowship to die with us.
This day is called the feast of Crispian;
He that outlives this day, and comes safe home,
Will stand a-tiptoe when this day is named,
And rouse him at the name of Crispian.
He that shall live this day and see old age,
Will yearly on the vigil feast his neighbours
And say "To-morrow is Saint Crispian"

Then he will strip his sleeve and show his scars
And say " These wounds I had on Crispian's day."

.   .   .   .   .

And gentlemen in England now a-bed
Shall think themselves accursed they were not here
And hold their manhoods cheap whiles any speaks
That fought with us upon St. Crispian's Day.

WILLIAM SHAKESPEARE.

Invictus

Out of the night that covers me
Black as the pit from pole to pole,
I thank whatever gods may be
For my unconquerable soul.

In the fell clutch of circumstance
I have not winced nor cried aloud.
Under the bludgeonings of chance
My head is bloody but unbowed.

It matters not how straight the gate
How charged with punishment the scroll,
I am the master of my fate,
I am the captain of my soul.

W. E. HENLEY.

Lepanto

Dim drums throbbing, in the hills half heard,
Where only on a nameless throne a crownless prince has
    stirred,
Where, risen from a doubtful seat and half-attainted stall,
The last knight of Europe takes weapons from the wall,

The last and lingering troubadour to whom the bird has sung,
That once went singing southward when all the world was
    young.
In that enormous silence, tiny and unafraid,
Comes up along a winding road the noise of the Crusade.
Strong gongs groaning as the guns boom far,
Don John of Austria is going to the war,
Stiff flags straining in the night-blasts cold
In the gloom black-purple, in the glint old-gold,
Torchlight crimson on the copper kettle-drums,
Then the tuckets, then the trumpets, then the cannon, and he
    comes.
Don John laughing in the brave beard curled,
Spurning of his stirrups like the thrones of all the world,
Holding his head up for a flag of all the free.
Love-light of Spain—hurrah!
Death-light of Africa!
Don John of Austria
Is riding to the sea.

G. K. CHESTERTON.

Into Battle

The naked earth is warm with spring,
    And with green grass and bursting trees
Leans to the sun's gaze glorying,
    And quivers in the sunny breeze;
And life is colour and warmth and light,
    And a striving evermore for these;
And he is dead who will not fight;
    And who dies fighting has increase.

The fighting man shall from the sun,
    Take warmth, and life from the glowing earth;
Speed with the light-foot winds to run,
    And with the trees to newer birth;

And find, when fighting shall be done,
  Great rest, and fullness after dearth.

All the bright company of Heaven,
  Hold him in their high comradeship,
The Dog-Star, and the Sisters Seven,
  Orion's Belt and sworded hip.

The woodland trees that stand together,
  They stand to him each one a friend;
They gently speak in the windy weather;
  They guide to valley and ridge's end.

The kestrel hovering by day,
  And the little owls that call by night,
Bid him be swift and keen as they,
  As keen of ear, as swift of sight.

The blackbird sings to him, " Brother, brother,
  If this be the last song you shall sing,
Sing well, for you may not sing another;
  Brother, sing."

In dreary, doubtful, waiting hours,
  Before the brazen frenzy starts,
The horses show him nobler powers;
  O patient eyes, courageous hearts!

And when the burning moment breaks,
  And all things else are out of mind,
And only joy of battle takes
  Him by the throat, and makes him blind.

Through joy and blindness he shall know
  Not caring much to know, that still
Nor lead nor steel shall reach him, so
  That it be not the Destined Will.

The thundering line of battle stands,
    And in the air death moans and sings;
But Day shall clasp him with strong hands,
    And Night shall fold him in soft wings.

JULIAN GRENFELL.

In Memoriam A. H.

Surely you found companions meet for you
In that high place;
You met there face to face
Those you had never known, but whom you knew;
Kinghts of the Table Round,
And all the very brave, the very true,
With chivalry crowned;
The captains rare,
Courteous and brave beyond our human air;
Those who had loved and suffered overmuch,
Now free from the world's touch.
And with them were the friends of yesterday,
Who went before and pointed you the way;
And in that place of freshness, light and rest,
Where Lancelot and Tristram vigil keep
Over their King's long sleep,
Surely they made a place for you,
Their long-expected guest,
Among the chosen few,
And welcomed you, their brother and their friend,
To that companionship which hath no end.

And in the portals of the sacred hall
You hear the trumpet's call,
At dawn upon the silvery battlement,
Re-echo through the deep
And bid the sons of God to rise from sleep

And with a shout to hail
The sunrise on the city of the Grail:
The music that proud Lucifer in Hell
Missed more than all the joys that he forwent
You hear the solemn bell
At vespers, when the oriflammes are furled;
And then you know that somewhere in the world,
That shines far-off beneath you like a gem,
They think of you, and when you think of them
You know that they will wipe away their tears,
And cast aside their fears;
That they will have it so,
And in no other wise;
That it is well with them because they know,
With faithful eyes,
Fixed forward and turned upwards to the skies,
That it is well with you,
Among the chosen few,
Among the very brave, the very true.

MAURICE BARING.

That the Night Come

She lived in storm and strife,
Her soul had such desire
For what proud death may bring
That it could not endure
The Common good of life,
But lived as 'twere a king
That packed his marriage day
With banneret and pennon,
Trumpet and kettledrum,
And the outrageous cannon,
To bundle time away
That the night come.

W. B. YEATS.

115

Last Lines

No coward soul is mine,
No trembler in the world's storm-troubled sphere:
   I see Heaven's glories shine,
And faith shines equal, arming me from fear.

O God within my breast,
Almighty, ever-present Deity!
   Life—that in me has rest,
As I—undying Life—have power in Thee!

Vain are the thousand creeds
That move men's hearts: unutterably vain;
   Worthless as wither'd weeds,
Or idlest froth amid the boundless main.

To waken doubt in one
Holding so fast by Thine infinity:
   So surely anchor'd on
The steadfast rock of immortality.

With wide embracing love
Thy Spirit animates eternal years,
   Pervades and broods above,
Changes, sustains, dissolves, creates, and rears.

Though earth and man were gone,
And suns and universes ceased to be,
   And Thou were left alone,
Every existence would exist in Thee.

There is not room for Death,
Nor atom that his might could render void:
   Thou—Thou art Being and Breath,
And what Thou art may never be destroy'd.

EMILY BRONTË.

A Ballad of Trees and the Master

Into the woods my Master went,
Clean forspent, forspent.
Into the woods my Master came,
Forspent with love and shame.
But the olives were not blind to Him,
The little grey leaves were kind to Him
The thorn-tree had a mind to Him
When into the woods He came.

Out of the woods my Master went,
And He was well content.
Out of the woods my Master came,
Content with death and shame.
When Death and shame would woo Him last,
From under the trees they drew Him last,
'Twas on a tree they slew Him—last
When out of the woods He came.

SIDNEY LANIER.

2 Corinthians, xi. 18

Seeing that many glory after the flesh, I will glory also.

2 Corinthians, xi. 21–31

I speak by way of disparagement, as though we had been weak. Yet whereinsoever any is bold (I speak in foolishness), I am bold also.

Are they Hebrews? so am I. Are they Israelites? so am I. Are they the seed of Abraham? so am I.

Are they ministers of Christ? (I speak as one beside himself) I more; in labours more abundantly, in prisons more abundantly, in stripes above measure, in deaths oft.

Of the Jews five times received I forty stripes save one.

Thrice was I beaten with rods, once was I stoned, thrice I suffered shipwreck, a night and a day have I been in the deep;

In journeyings often, in perils of rivers, in perils of robbers, in perils from my countrymen, in perils from the Gentiles, in perils in the city, in perils in the wilderness, in perils in the sea, in perils among false brethren;

In labour and travail, in watchings often, in hunger and thirst, in fastings often, in cold and nakedness.

Beside those things that are without, there is that which presseth upon me daily, anxiety for all the churches.

Who is weak, and I am not weak? who is made to stumble, and I burn not?

If I must needs glory, I will glory of the things that concern my weakness.

The God and Father of the Lord Jesus, he who is blessed for evermore, knoweth that I lie not.

Epilogue

At the midnight in the silence of the sleep-time,
    When you set your fancies free,
Will they pass to where—by death, fools think, imprisoned—
    Here he lies who once so loved you, whom you loved so,
            —Pity me?

O to love so, be so loved. Yet so mistaken!
    What had I on earth to do
With the slothful, with the mawkish, the unmanly?
    Like the aimless, helpless, hopeless, did I drivel
            —Being—Who?

118

One who never turned his back but marched breast forward,
　Never doubted clouds would break,
Never dreamed, though right were worsted, wrong would
　　triumph,
　Held we fall to rise, are baffled to fight better,
　　　　Sleep to wake.

No, at noonday in the bustle of man's worktime
　Greet the unseen with a cheer !
Bid him forward, breast and back as either should be
　" Strive and thrive ! " cry " Speed,—fight on, fare ever
　　　　There as here."

ROBERT BROWNING.

PART NINE

SORROW

Producer:

H. ROSE.

Speakers:

ROBERT HARRIS.

[*By kind permission of St. Martin's Theatre Management.*]

JOHN LAURIE.

[*By kind permission of Sydney Carroll.*]

Music:

Selected by H. FOSTER CLARK.

" In a Summer Garden " (Delius). H.M.V. D1696.

" In a Summer Garden " (Delius). H.M.V. D1697.

PROLOGUE

SORROW is in part happiness lost and recollected in tranquillity. Grief is swift, violent, and, if expressed in colour, black; but sorrow is grey and lays gentle hands on tired eyes. The pilgrim steps out of the great highway of delight into the shade of sorrow. It is at first almost grateful to the over-tired sense. Soon, however, creeps upon the mind the cold touch of loss. In the grey undertones there is the memory of what was bright, kind and gay.

In the voice of the nightingale sorrow falls through ecstasy into tears. Here she assumes the proud shape of beauty, and prevails upon time. Her other name is memory—of all that was fair and kindly, and will not come again. It is now the sob of women whose men have gone brilliant into death and who have robbed the spring of blossom. It is the sigh of friendship mourning the dear head that winter ravished. It has the slow sweep and agony of the retreating tide, in whose cold deep there drowns the irrecoverable beloved. And it is the lament of inevitable fate—that all grows weary, all passes, all in the end breaks and crumbles.

Sorrow comes on gentle foot, and at her side paces comfort. Nature leans down to her with the consolation of the rain and the white sacring of the snow. Here are small and gentle hands laid in blessing on the bended brow. While far beyond the limits of the world, epitome of sorrow, transmuted into joy everlasting, trembles the dim figure whose darkness and whose sorrow are all our light and our enfranchisement.

From " Il Penseroso "

Hence vain deluding joyes,
　The Brood of folly without father bred,
How little you bested,
　Or fill the fixed mind with all your toyes;
Dwell in som idle brain,
　And fancies fond with gaudy shapes possess,
As thick and numberless
　As the gay motes that people the Sun Beams,
Or likest hovering dreams
　The fickle Pensioners of Morpheus train.
But hail thou Goddess, sage and holy,
Hail divinest Melancholy,
Whose Saintly visage is too bright
To hit the Sense of human sight;
And therefore to our weaker view,
Ore laid with black staid Wisdoms hue.

JOHN MILTON.

Rarely, Rarely, Comest Thou

Rarely, rarely, comest thou,
　　Spirit of Delight!
Wherefore has thou left me now
　　Many a day and night?
Many a weary night and day
'Tis since thou art fled away.

How shall ever one like me
　　Win thee back again?
With the joyous and the free
　　Thou wilt scoff at pain.
Spirit false! thou has forgot
All but those who need thee not.

As a lizard with the shade
    Of a trembling leaf,
Thou with sorrow art dismayed;
    Even the sighs of grief
Reproach thee, that thou art not near,
And reproach thou wilt not hear.

Let me set my mournful ditty
    To a merry measure;
Thou wilt never come for pity,
    Thou wilt come for pleasure;
Pity then will cut away,
Those cruel wings, and thou wilt stay.

PERCY BYSSHE SHELLEY.

Philomela

Hark! ah, the Nightingale!
    The tawny-throated!
Hark! from that moonlit cedar what a burst!
What triumph! hark—what pain!

O Wanderer from a Grecian shore,
Still, after many years, in distant lands,
Still nourishing in thy bewilder'd brain
That wild, unquench'd, deep-sunken, old-world pain—
    Say, will it never heal?
And can this fragrant lawn
With its cool trees, and night,
And the sweet, tranquil Thames,
And moonshine, and the dew,
To thy rack'd heart and brain
    Afford no balm?

Dost thou to-night behold
Here, through the moonlight on this English grass,
The unfriendly palace in the Thracian wild?
Dost thou again peruse
With hot cheeks and sear'd eyes
The too clear web, and thy dumb Sister's shame?
Dost thou once more assay
Thy flight, and feel come over thee,
Poor Fugitive, the feathery change
Once more, and once more seem to make resound
With love and hate, triumph and agony,
Lone Daulis, and the high Cephissian vale?
Listen, Eugenia—
How thick the bursts come crowding through the leaves!
Again—thou hearest!
Eternal Passion!
Eternal Pain!

MATTHEW ARNOLD.

A Daughter of Eve

A Fool I was to sleep at noon
And wake when night is chilly
Beneath the comfortless cold moon;
A fool to pluck my rose too soon,
A fool to snap my lily.

My garden-plot I have not kept;
Faded and all forsaken,
I weep as I have never wept:
Oh it was summer when I slept,
It's winter now I waken.

Talk what you please of future Spring
And sun-warmed sweet to-morrow:—

126

Stripped bare of hope and everything,
No more to laugh, no more to sing,
  I sit alone with sorrow.
            CHRISTINA ROSSETTI.

Tears, Idle Tears

Tears, idle tears, I know not what they mean,
Tears from the depth of some divine despair
Rise in the heart, and gather to the eyes,
In looking on the happy autumn fields,
And thinking of the days that are no more.

Fresh as the first beam glittering on a sail,
That brings our friends up from the underworld,
Sad as the last which reddens over one
That sinks with all we love below the verge;
So sad, so fresh, the days that are no more.

Ah, sad and strange as in dark summer dawns
The earliest pipe of half-awaken'd birds
To dying ears, when unto dying eyes
The casement slowly grows a glimmering square;
So sad, so strange, the days that are no more.

Dear as remember'd kisses after death,
And sweet as those by hopeless fancy feign'd
On lips that are for others; deep as love,
Deep as first love, and wild with all regret;
O Death in Life, the days that are no more.
            TENNYSON.

A Lament for Flodden

I've heard them lilting at our ewe-milking,
    Lasses a' lilting before dawn o' day;
But now they are moaning on ilka green loaning—
    The Flowers of the Forest are a' wede away.

At bughts, in the morning, nae blythe lads are scorning,
    Lasses are lonely and dowie and wae;
Nae daffing, nae gabbing, but sighing and sabbing,
    Ilk ane lifts her leglin and hies her away.

In har'st, at the shearing, nae youths now are jeering,
    Bandsters are lyart, and runkled, and gray:
At fair or at preaching, nae wooing, nae fleeching—
    The Flowers of the Forest are a' wede away.

At e'en, in the gloaming, nae swankies are roaming
    'Bout stacks wi' the lasses at bogle to play;
But ilk ane sits eerie, lamenting her dearie—
    The Flowers of the Forest are a' wede away.

Dool and wae for the order sent our lads to the Border!
    The English, for ance, by guile wan the day;
The Flowers of the Forest, that fought aye the foremost,
    The prime of our land, lie cauld in the clay.

We'll hear nae mair lilting at our ewe-milking;
    Women and bairns are heartless and wae;
Sighing and moaning on ilka green loaning—
    The Flowers of the Forest are a' wede away.

JANE ELLIOT.

Echo's Lament for Narcissus

Slow, slow, fresh fount, keep time with my salt tears;
   Yet, slower yet; O faintly, gentle springs;
List to the heavy part the music bears;
   Woe weeps out her division when she sings.
   Droop herbs and flowers;
   Fall grief in showers,
   Our beauties are not ours;
     O, I could still,
Like melting snow upon some craggy hill,
   Drop, drop, drop, drop,
Since nature's pride is now a withered daffodil.

                BEN JONSON.

I Never Shall Love the Snow Again

I never shall love the snow again
   Since Maurice died:
With corniced drift it blocked the lane
And sheeted in a desolate plain
   The country side.

The trees with silvery rime bedight
   Their branches bare.
By day no sun appeared; by night
The hidden moon shed thievish light
   In the misty air.

We fed the birds that flew around
   In flocks to be fed:
No shelter in holly or brake they found.
The speckled thrush on the frozen ground
   Lay frozen and dead.

We skated on stream and pond; we cut
    The crinching snow
To Doric temple or Arctic hut;
We laughed and sang at nightfall, shut
    By the fireside glow.

Yet grudged we our keen delights before
    Maurice should come
We said, in-door or out-of-door
We shall love life for a month or more,
    When he is home.

They brought him home; 'twas two days late
    For Christmas day:
Wrapped in white, in solemn state,
A flower in his hand, all still and straight
    Our Maurice lay.

And two days ere the year outgave
    We laid him low.
The best of us truly were not brave,
When we laid Maurice down in his grave
    Under the snow.

                   ROBERT BRIDGES.

From " The High Tide on the Coast of Lincolnshire, 1571 "

The old mayor climb'd the belfry tower
    The ringers ran by two, by three;
" Pull, if ye never pull'd before;
    Good ringers, pull your best," quoth he.
" Play uppe, play uppe, O Boston bells!
Ply all your changes, all your swells,
    Play uppe ' The Brides of Enderby '."

Men say it was a stolen tyde—
    The Lord that sent it, He knows all;
But in myne ears doth still abide
    The message that the bells let fall:
And there was naught of strange, beside
The flights of mews and peewits pied
    By millions crouch'd on the old sea wall.

I sat and spun within the doore,
    My thread brake off, I raised myne eyes;
The level sun, like ruddy ore,
    Lay sinking in the barren skies,
And dark against day's golden death
She moved where Lindis wandereth,
    My sonne's fair wife, Elizabeth.

" Cusha! Cusha! Cusha!" calling,
Ere the early dews were falling,
Farre away I heard her song.
    " Cusha! Cusha!" all along
Where the reedy Lindis floweth,
        Floweth, floweth;
From the meads where melick groweth
    Faintly came her milking song—

JEAN INGELOW.

The Old Familiar Faces

I have had playmates, I have had companions,
In my days of childhood, in my joyful school-days—
All, all are gone, the old familiar faces.

I have been laughing, I have been carousing,
Drinking late, sitting late, with my bosom cronies—
All, all are gone, the old familiar faces.

I loved a Love once, fairest among women:
Closed are her doors on me, I must not see her—
All, all are gone, the old familiar faces.

I have a friend, a kinder friend has no man:
Like an ingrate, I left my friend abruptly;
Left him, to muse on the old familiar faces.

Ghost-like I paced the haunts of my childhood,
Earth seem'd a desert I was bound to traverse,
Seeking to find the old familiar faces.

Friend of my bosom, thou more than a brother,
Why were not thou born in my father's dwelling?
So might we talk of the old familiar faces—

How some they have died, and some they have left me,
And some are taken from me; all are departed—
All, all are gone, the old familiar faces.

CHARLES LAMB.

The Comforters

When I crept over the hill, broken with tears,
    When I crouched down on the grass, dumb in despair,
I heard the soft croon of the wind bend to my ears,
    I felt the light kiss of the wind touching my hair.

When I stood lone on the height my sorrow did speak,
    As I went down the hill, I cried and I cried,
The soft little hands of the rain stroking my cheek,
    The kind little feet of the rain ran by my side.

When I went to thy grave, broken with tears,
    When I crouched down in the grass, dumb in despair,
I heard the sweet croon of the wind soft in my ears,
    I felt the kind lips of the wind touching my hair.

When I stood lone by thy cross, sorrow did speak,
  When I went down the long hill, I cried and I cried,
The soft little hands of the rain stroked my pale cheek,
  The kind little feet of the rain ran by my side.

DORA SIGERSON SHORTER.

Moving through the Silent Crowd

Moving through the silent crowd
Who stand behind dull cigarettes
These men who idle in the road,
I have the sense of falling light.

They lounge at corners of the street
And greet friends with a shrug of shoulder
And turn their empty pockets out,
The cynical gestures of the poor.

Now they've no work, like better men
Who sit at desks and take much pay
They sleep long nights and rise at ten
To watch the hours that drain away.

I'm jealous of the weeping hours
They stare through with such hungry eyes.
I'm haunted by these images,
I'm haunted by their emptiness.

STEPHEN SPENDER.

He is the Lonely Greatness

He is the lonely greatness of the world—
    (His eyes are dim),
His power it is holds up the Cross
    That holds up Him.

133

He takes the sorrow of the threefold hour—
    (His eyelids close),
Round him and round, the wind—His Spirit—where
    It listeth blows.

And so the wounded greatness of the World
    In silence lies—
And death is shattered by the light from out
    Those darkened eyes.

MADELEINE CARON ROCK.

PART TEN

TEMPTATION

Producer:

Miss M. H. ALLEN.

Speakers:

ION SWINLEY.

ROBERT SPEAIGHT.

Music:

Selected by MAURICE BROWN.

"Classical" Symphony, in D Minor (Prokofieff), 1st, 2nd and 3rd Movements.   H.M.V. D1857.

Overture in D Minor (Handel, *arr.* Elgar).
                                          H.M.V. D1527.

"Origin of Design" (Handel, *arr.* Beecham).
                                          Columbia LX224.

"Daphnis and Chloe" (Ravel).   H.M.V. D1826.

"Antar" (Rimsky Korsakov).   H.M.V. DB4889.

"Firebird," Danse Infernale (Stravinsky).
                                          H.M.V. D1510.

PROLOGUE

THERE are many voices of temptation, the glittering serpent that Eve admitted to all our hearts. The subtlest eft offers all things to all men, above all reward without labour, sin without punishment. At the beginning of the world he offered the end of peace to Eve lapped in the innocence of God. By her acceptance—poor mother Eve, poor girl in her orchard—she lost tranquillity for mankind in exchange for the unconquerable hope for the impossible.

That is still a sharp lure. To escape from simplicity into action, to leave the country of quiet for the town of mental strife, to believe that to do is better than to be—here still sounds the voice that urged the apple. That is the trap for the subtle, the last infirmity of noble minds. For those less delicate there is the Siren's voice, bidding the Pilgrim dash his bark upon the Lorelei's rock, and so founder. Or it may call with the Persian to leave all desire save that of the moment. "Gather ye rosebuds while ye may," comes the sweet swift whisper to the pilgrim. Difficult to resist in the time of roses, though how often when the pilgrim has dared and lost all for the inaccessible Helen, must he return, old and weary, to his own soul, regretting the lost delights that were brief, and in remembrance how bitter.

But there is a more dangerous temptation yet—the bid of refusal. Why should the pilgrim moil and toil when there are rest and marvel in the opium radiance of dream? There the pilgrim can build—unhindered and unhelped—his pleasure-dome. There he can hear music, sweeter because it is shared with none, and there he can feed on the honey-dew of victory without sweat, and wear the laurel before ever the race be run. Yes, that is a clear and a perilous call—to lay the world away and hear the old imagined gods wind the pagan horn that scatters all truth upon the wind.

Yet, if temptation be both various and cunning, it is possible to know its nature and to resist it. For how shall the pilgrim prevail if he does not encounter the dust and the heat? Shall he not rather say " Give me temptation, and I will show you a man "? The City of Vanity Fair winks to him with its thousand brilliant booths, but he will remember one who refused all the Kingdoms of the Earth. So comes the temptation of Nirvana, of the dreamless end of all. " Come unto me," mocks the devil, misquoting scripture to his purpose, " and I will give you peace." And in that moment Christ in the soul of man rises and makes answer, " I know you, devil, and I know you lie."

Eve

Eve, with her basket, was
Deep in the bells and grass
Wading in bells and grass
Up to her knees,
Picking a dish of sweet
Berries and plums to eat,
Down in the bells and grass
Under the trees.

Mute as a mouse in a
Corner the cobra lay,
Curled round a bough of the
Cinnamon tal. . . .
Now to get even and
Humble proud heaven and
Now was the moment or
Never at all.

" Eva ! " Each syllable
Light as a flower fell,
" Eva ! " he whispered the
Wondering maid,
Soft as a bubble sung
Out of a linnet's lung,
Soft and most silverly
" Eva ! " he said.

Picture that orchard sprite,
Eve, with her body white,
Supple and smooth to her
Slim finger-tips,
Wondering, listening,
Listening, wondering,

Eve with a berry
Half-way to her lips.

Oh had our simple Eve
Seen through the make-believe!
Had she but known the
Pretender he was!
Out of the boughs he came,
Whispering still her name,
Tumbling in twenty rings
Into the grass.

Here was the strangest pair
In the world anywhere,
Eve in the bells and grass
Kneeling, and he
Telling his story low . . .
Singing birds saw them go
Down the dark path to
The Blasphemous Tree.

Oh what a clatter when
Titmouse and Jenny Wren
Saw him successful and
Taking his leave!
How the birds rated him,
How they all hated him!
How they all pitied
Poor motherless Eve!

Picture her crying
Outside in the lane,
Eve, with no dish of sweet
Berries and plums to eat,
Haunting the gate of the
Orchard in vain. . . .

Picture the lewd delight
Under the hill tonight—
" Eva ! " the toast goes round,
" Eva ! " again.

RALPH HODGSON.

From " Paradise Lost "

Great are thy Vertues, doubtless, best of Fruits
Though kept from Man, and worthy to be admir'd,
Whose taste, too long forborn, at first assay
Gave elocution to the mute, and taught
The Tongue not made for Speech to speak thy praise :
Thy praise hee also who forbids thy use,
Conceales not from us, naming thee the Tree
Of Knowledge, knowledge both of good and evil;
Forbids us then to taste, but his forbidding
Commends thee more, while it inferrs the good
By thee communicated, and our want :
For good unknown, sure is not had, or had
And yet unknown, is as not had at all.
In plain then, what forbide he but to know,
Forbids us good, forbids us to be wise?
Such prohibitions binde not.   But if Death
Bind us with after-bands, what profits then
Our inward freedom?   In the day we eate
Of this fair Fruit, our doom is, we shall die.
How dies the Serpent? hee hath eat'n and lives,
And knows, and speaks, and reasons, and discernes,
Irrational till then.   For us alone
Was death invented?   or to us deni'd
This intellectual food, for beasts reserv'd?
For beasts it seems :   yet that one Beast which first
Hath tasted, envies not, but brings with joy
The good befall'n him, Author unsuspect,

141

Friendly to man, farr from deceit or guile.
What fear I then, rather what know to feare
Under this ignorance of Good and Evil,
Of God or Death, of Law or Penaltie?
Here grows the cure of all, this Fruit Divine,
Fair to the Eye, inviting to the Taste,
Of vertue to make wise: what hinders then
To reach, and feed at once both Bodie and Mind?

So saying, her rash hand in evil hour
Forth reaching to the Fruit, she pluck'd, she eat:
Earth felt the wound, and Nature from her seat
Sighing through all her Works gave signs of woe,
That all was lost. Back to the Thicket slunk
The guiltie Serpent, and well might, for *Eve*
Intent now wholly on her taste, naught else
Regarded, such delight till then, as seem'd,
In Fruit she never tasted, whether true
Or fansied so, through expectation high
Of knowledge, nor was God-head from her thought.
Greedily she ingorg'd without restraint,
And knew not eating Death.

JOHN MILTON.

The Sirens' Song

Steer, hither steer your wingèd pines,
    All beaten mariners!
Here lie Love's undiscover'd mines,
    A prey to passengers—
Perfumes far sweeter than the best
Which make the Phœnix' urn and nest.
    Fear not your ships,
Nor any to oppose you save our lips;
    But come on shore,
Where no joy dies till Love hath gotten more.

For swelling waves our panting breasts,
    Where never storms arise,
Exchange, and be awhile our guests:
    For stars gaze on our eyes.
The compass Love shall hourly sing,
And as he goes about the ring,
    We will not miss
To tell each point he nameth with a kiss.
    —Then come on shore,
Where no joy dies till Love hath gotten more.

WILLIAM BROWNE.

From " The Rubaiyat of Omar Khayyam "

Come, fill the Cup, and in the fire of Spring
Your Winter-garment of Repentance fling:
    The Bird of Time has but a little way
To flutter—and the Bird is on the Wing.

Each Morn a thousand Roses brings, you say;
Yes, but where leaves the Rose of Yesterday?
    And this first Summer month that brings the Rose
Shall take Jamshýd and Kaikobád away.

Well, let it take them! What have we to do
With Kaikobád the Great, or Kaikhosrú?
    Let Zál and Rustam bluster as they will
Or Hátim call to Supper—heed not you.

With me along the strip of Herbage strown
That just divides the desert from the sown
    Where name of Slave and Sultán is forgot—
And Peace to Mahmúd on his golden Throne!

143

A Book of Verses underneath the Bough,
A Jug of Wine, a Loaf of Bread—and Thou
  Beside me singing in the Wilderness—
Oh, Wilderness were Paradise enow!

Some for the Glories of This World; and some
Sigh for the Prophet's Paradise to come;
  Ah, take the Cash, and let the Credit go,
Nor heed the rumble of a distant Drum!

Look to the blowing Rose about us—" Lo,
Laughing," she says, " into the world I blow,
  At once the silken tassel of my Purse
Tear, and its Treasure on the Garden throw."

The Worldly Hope men set their Hearts upon
Turns Ashes—or it prospers; and anon,
  Like Snow upon the Desert's dusty Face,
Lighting a little hour or two—is gone.

They say the Lion and the Lizard keep
The Courts where Jamshýd gloried and drank deep:
  And Bahrám, that great Hunter—the Wild Ass
Stamps o'er his Head, but cannot break his Sleep.

I sometimes think that never blows so red
The Rose as where some buried Cæsar bled;
  That every Hyacinth the Garden wears
Dropt in her Lap from some once lovely Head.

And this reviving Herb whose tender Green
Fledges the River-Lip on which we lean—
  Ah, lean upon it lightly! for who knows
From what once lovely Lip it springs unseen!

Ah, my Belovéd, fill the Cup that clears
To-DAY of past Regrets and Future Fears:
  To-morrow!—Why, To-morrow I may be
Myself with Yesterday's Sev'n thousand Years.

For some we loved, the loveliest and the best
That from his Vintage rolling Time hath prest,
　　Have drunk their Cup a round or two before,
And one by one crept silently to rest.

And we, that now make merry in the Room
They left, and Summer dresses in new bloom,
　　Ourselves must we beneath the Couch of Earth
Descend—ourselves to make a Couch—for whom?

Ah, make the most of what we yet may spend,
Before we too into the Dust descend;
　　Dust into Dust, and under Dust to lie
Sans Wine, sans Song, sans Singer, and—sans End!

EDWARD FITZGERALD.

From " Doctor Faustus "

Was this the face that launch'd a thousand ships,
And burnt the topless towers of Ilium?
Sweet Helen, make me immortal with a kiss.

Her lips suck forth my soul: see, where it flies!—
Come, Helen, come, give me my soul again.
Here will I dwell, for heaven is in these lips,
And all is dross that is not Helena.
I will be Paris, and for love of thee,
Instead of Troy, shall Wertenberg be sack'd;
And I will combat with weak Menelaus,
And wear thy colours on my plumed crest;
Yes, I will wound Achilles in the heel,
And then return to Helen for a kiss.
O, thou art fairer than the evening air
Clad in the beauty of a thousand stars;
Brighter art thou than flaming Jupiter
When he appear'd to hapless Semele;

More lovely than the monarch of the sky
In wanton Arethusa's azur'd arms;
And none but thou shalt be my paramour!

CHRISTOPHER MARLOWE.

We'll go no more A-Roving

So, we'll go no more a-roving
    So late into the night,
Though the heart be still as loving
    And the moon be still as bright.

For the sword outwears its sheath,
    And the soul wears out the breast,
And the heart must pause to breathe,
    And love itself have rest.

Though the night was made for loving
    And the day returns too soon,
Yet we'll go no more a-roving
    By the light of the moon.

BYRON.

From " The Lotus-Eaters "

There is sweet music here that softer falls
Than petals from blown roses on the grass,
Or night-dews on still waters between walls
Of shadowy granite, in a gleaming pass;
Music that gentlier on the spirit lies,
Than tired eyelids upon tired eyes;
Music that brings sweet sleep down from the blissful
    skies.
Here are cool mosses deep,
And thro' the moss the ivies creep,
And in the stream the long-leaved flowers weep,
And from the craggy ledge the poppy hangs in sleep.

Why are we weigh'd upon with heaviness,
And utterly consumed with sharp distress,
While all things else have rest from weariness?
All things have rest: why should we toil alone,
We only toil, who are the first of things,
And make perpetual moan,
Still from one sorrow to another thrown:
Nor ever fold our wings,
And cease from wanderings,
Nor steep our brows in slumber's holy balm;
Nor hearken what the inner spirit sings,
"There is no joy but calm!"—
Why should we only toil, the roof and crown of
        things?

Lo! in the middle of the wood,
The folded leaf is woo'd from out the bud
With winds upon the branch, and there
Grows green and broad, and takes no care,
Sun-steep'd at noon, and in the moon
Nightly dew-fed; and turning yellow
Falls, and floats adown the air.
Lo! sweeten'd with the summer light,
The full-juiced apple, waxing over-mellow,
Drops in a silent autumn night.
All its allotted length of days,
The flower ripens in its place,
Ripens and fades, and falls, and hath no toil,
Fast-rooted in the fruitful soil.

Hateful is the dark-blue sky,
Vaulted o'er the dark-blue sea.
Death is the end of life; ah, why
Should life all labour be?
Let us alone. Time driveth onward fast,
And in a little while our lips are dumb.
Let us alone. What is it that will last?

All things are taken from us, and become
Portions and parcels of the dreadful Past.
Let us alone.   What pleasure can we have
To war with evil?   Is there any peace
In ever climbing up the climbing wave?
All things have rest, and ripen toward the grave
In silence; ripen, fall and cease:
Give us long rest or death, dark death, or dreamful
　　ease.

TENNYSON.

Kubla Khan

In Xanadu did Kubla Khan
　A stately pleasure dome decree:
Where Alph, the sacred river, ran
Through caverns measureless to man
　Down to the sunless sea.
So twice five miles of fertile ground
　With walls and towers were girdled round:
And there were gardens bright with sinuous rills
Where blossom'd many an incense bearing tree;
And here were forests ancient as the hills,
Enfolding sunny spots of greenery.

But O, that deep romantic chasm which slanted
Down the green hill athwart a cedarn cover!
A savage place! as holy and enchanted
As e'er beneath a waning moon was haunted
By woman wailing for her demon-lover!
And from this chasm, with ceaseless turmoil seething,
As if this earth in fast thick pants were breathing,
A mighty fountain momently was forced;
Amid whose swift half-intermitted burst
Huge fragments vaulted like rebounding hail,
Or chaffy grain beneath the thresher's flail:

And 'mid these dancing rocks at once and ever
It flung up momently the sacred river.
Five miles meandering with a mazy motion
Through wood and dale the sacred river ran,
Then reach'd the caverns measureless to man,
And sank in tumult to a lifeless ocean:
And mid this tumult Kubla heard from far
Ancestral voices prophesying war!
    The shadow of the dome of pleasure
        Floated midway on the waves;
    Where was heard the mingled measure
        From the fountain and the caves.
It was a miracle of rare device,
A sunny pleasure dome with caves of ice!

    A damsel with a dulcimer
        In a vision once I saw:
    It was an Abyssinian maid,
        And on her dulcimer she play'd,
    Singing of Mount Abora.

    Could I revive within me,
        Her symphony and song,
To such delight 't would win me,
That with music loud and long,
I would build that dome in air,
That sunny dome! those caves of ice!
And all who heard should see them there,
And all should cry, Beware! Beware!
His flashing eyes, his floating hair!
Weave a circle round him thrice,
    And close your eyes with holy dread,
    For he on honey-dew hath fed,
And drunk the milk of Paradise.

                    SAMUEL TAYLOR COLERIDGE.

149

The World

The world is too much with us; late and soon,
    Getting and spending, we lay waste our powers;
  Little we see in Nature that is ours;
We have given our hearts away, a sordid boon:
This sea that bares her bosom to the moon;
    The winds that will be howling at all hours,
    And are up-gather'd now like sleeping flowers;
For this, for everything, we are out of tune;
It moves us not.—Great God! I'd rather be
    A Pagan suckled in a creed outworn;
So might I, standing on this pleasant lea,
    Have glimpses that would make me less forlorn;
Have sight of Proteus rising from the sea;
    Or hear old Triton blow his wreathèd horn.

WILLIAM WORDSWORTH.

From " The General Epistle of James "

Count it all joy, my brethren when ye fall into manifold temptations; Knowing that the proof of your faith worketh patience. And let patience have its perfect work, that ye may be perfect and entire, lacking in nothing.

Let no man say when he is tempted, I am tempted of God: for God cannot be tempted with evil, and he himself tempteth no man: But each man is tempted, when he is drawn away by his own lust, and enticed. Then the lust, when it hath conceived, beareth sin: and the sin, when it is full-grown, bringeth forth death.

From " The Ring and the Book "

Why comes temptation but for man to meet
And master and make crouch beneath his foot,
And so be pedestalled in triumph? Pray
" Lead us into no such temptations, Lord! "
Yea, but, O Thou whose servants are the bold,
Lead such temptations by the head and hair,
Reluctant dragons, up to who dares fight,
That so he may do battle and have praise!

ROBERT BROWNING.

From " Pilgrim's Progress "

Then I saw in my dream, that when they were got out of
the wilderness, they presently saw a town before them, and
the name of that town is Vanity; and at the town there is a
fair kept, called Vanity Fair. It is kept all the year long. It
beareth the name of Vanity Fair, because the town where it
is kept is lighter than vanity; and also, because all that is
there sold, or that cometh thither, is vanity, as is the saying
of the wise, All that cometh is vanity.

. . . . .

Now, as I said the way to the Celestial City lies just through
this town where this lusty fair is kept; and he who will go
to the city and yet not go through this town, must needs go
out of the world. The Prince of princes Himself, when here,
went through this town to His own country, and that upon
a fair-day too; yea, and, as I think, it was Beelzebub, the
chief lord of this fair, that invited Him to buy of his vanities,
yea, would have made Him lord of the fair, would He but
have done him reverence as He went through the town.
Yea, because He was such a person of honour, Beelzebub
had Him from street to street, and showed Him all the

kingdoms of the world in a little time, that he might, if possible, allure that Blessed One to cheapen and buy some of his vanities; but He had no mind to the merchandise, and, therefore, left the town without laying out so much as one farthing upon these vanities.

JOHN BUNYAN.

From " News of the Devil "

And now the devil's voice rose up and out,
like the last trumpet in an army's rout
" Dust are the stars, and mankind's deepest lust
only a lazy wind that stirs the dust,
and dies again, leaving the dust as level
whether it blew from God or from the devil.
And neither God nor devil knows or cares
how dust may regulate its grey affairs,
since what men call the devil, and their sense
of God, is mankind's last impertinence.
This is self-knowledge, Arthur. Say you sinned,
it is the same as goodness in the end.
What shall it matter if a grain of dust
fulfils its mission or its interest,
since all its interest or mission is,
starting with nameless dust, to end with this?
And say one grain of dust dominion gains
over a thousand, no a myriad grains,
it is no more than if a rain-drop tried
shoreward to drag the whole Atlantic tide.
It does not change the other grains, or even
change its own doom, not made in Hell or Heaven,
but in the long decay of the first thought
that slowly crumbles backward into naught.
Grain rubs on grain, and as they work and fester,
contemptuous Time, unconscious, pricks the blister,

God is not mocked, Paul Arthur, by the dust,
and you will mingle quiet with the rest,
as undistinguishable and as small
as though you had not lived or died at all.
Be not afraid, all that you were, and are,
is but the putrefaction of a star,
and nothing that you could have done, or can,
could change the grovelling destiny of man."

Then something in Paul Arthur rose to cry
"I know you, devil, and I know you lie. . . ."

HUMBERT WOLFE.

PART ELEVEN

WORSHIP

Producer:

Miss M. H. ALLEN.

Speakers:

ROBERT SPEAIGHT.

ROBERT HARRIS.

[*By kind permission of St. Martin's Theatre Management.*]

Music:

Selected by MAURICE BROWN.

Organ Concerto in B Flat (Handel), 1st Movement.
                                    H.M.V. B2890.

Sinfonia, Church Cantata, No. 156 (Bach).
                                    Columbia DB506.

Concerto Grosso, No. 8 (Corelli) (" Christmas Concerto ").
                                    Parlophone E11065.

Symphony, No. 5 (Schubert), Menuetto.   Decca CA8162.

Symphony, No. 5 (Schubert), Andante con moto.
                                    Decca CA8162.

Organ Concerto in B Flat (Handel), 2nd and 3rd Movements.   H.M.V. B2891.

Choral Prelude, " Christ lay in bonds of death " (Bach).
                                    H.M.V. DB1952.

Variations on a Theme by Haydn (Brahms).
                                    H.M.V. D1377.

Dream of Gerontius (" And now the threshold ") (Elgar).
                                    H.M.V. D1242.

Piano Concerto in B Flat (Brahms), 1st Movement.
                                    H.M.V. D1746.

Chorale, " If I should e'er forsake Thee " (Bach).
                                    H.M.V. C2252.

PROLOGUE

The spirit of man may be likened to a broken arc, which points beyond itself to the completed circle. He has no power over his limitation which is imposed from beyond the world, but its essence is to reach out to the unlimited and unconstrained. This passionate desire for the whole, for the everlasting, for the unspotted and the unchangeable is in all men, even the worst or the most savage, implicit, and its name is worship.

To a very few among the pilgrims of earth there is vouchsafed the direct object of worship. So Isaiah, conscious of his manifold imperfections, beheld the King enthroned with his bright courtiers. So the beloved Vaughan was aware of eternity as the complete and brilliant circle tow hich its broken segments aspire.

But worship is not always in and through the vision of ultimate beauty. It may come with Easter flowers or, as with Ralph Hodgson, in the sweet-smelling mystery of the rose. Or it may express itself in joy at God's infinite variety—in the stipple of the trout, fresh fire-coal and chestnut-falls. In turning from this natural exaltation worship may be sweet with all regret, and of its strength may kiss the rod of darkness, crying magnificently :

" Dear beauteous death, the jewel of the just."

The saints see face to face; the pilgrims on the way see through a glass darkly, but the darkness of some is lit with distant silver. The soul may lift its branches to the shrine or ascend thither by the sunbeam's path. And some of the adventurers, though they may be benighted by life, yet can hear the overtones of light. The diapason of great song may reach where the singer cannot follow. The heavens may be splendid with the fire of music, while the poet stands, lonely, blinded with the stars that he has touched but cannot see.

But at the end worship, attaining the lion-glory of the Revelation, loud as a long trumpet, peals the triumph and the reward. The words surpass themselves, bearing a greater weight than their own, and shaken free in an absolute diction, untrammelled by dark or doubt, there is heard the last benediction: " Blessing, and glory, and wisdom, and thanksgiving, and honour and power, and might be unto our God for ever and ever. AMEN."

Isaiah vi. 1–5

In the year that King Uzziah died I saw the Lord sitting upon a throne, high and lifted up, and His train filled the temple. Above Him stood the seraphim: each one had six wings; with twain he covered his face, and with twain he covered his feet, and with twain he did fly. And one cried unto another, and said, Holy, holy, holy, is the Lord of Hosts: the whole earth is full of His glory. And the foundations of the thresholds were moved at the voice of him that cried, and the house was filled with smoke. Then said I, Woe is me! for I am undone; because I am a man of unclean lips, and I dwell in the midst of a people of unclean lips: for mine eyes have seen the King, the Lord of Hosts.

A Vision

I saw Eternity the other night,
Like a great ring of pure and endless light,
   All calm, as it was bright:—
And round beneath it, Time, in hours, days, years,
   Driven by the spheres,
Like a vast shadow moved; in which the World
   And all her train were hurl'd.

HENRY VAUGHAN.

Easter

I got me flowers to strew thy way,
   I got me boughs off many a tree;
But Thou wast up by break of day,
   And brought'st thy sweets along with Thee.

Yet though my flowers be lost, they say
  A heart can never come too late:
Teach it to sing Thy praise this day,
  And then this day my life shall date.

GEORGE HERBERT.

The Mystery

He came and took me by the hand
  Up to a red rose-tree,
He kept his meaning to Himself
  But gave a rose to me.

I did but pray Him to lay bare
  The mystery to me;
Enough, the rose was Heaven to smell,
  And His own face to see.

RALPH HODGSON.

Pied Beauty

Glory be to God for dappled things—
  For skies as couple-coloured as a brindled cow;
    For rose-moles all in stipple upon trout that swim;
Fresh fire-coal, chestnut-falls; finches' wings
  Landscapes plotted and pieced-fold, fallow and plough;
    And all trades, their gear and tackle and trim.
All things counter, original, spare, strange;
  Whatever is fickle, freckled (who knows how?)
    With swift, slow; sweet, sour; dazzle, dim;
He gathers-forth whose beauty is past change:
        Praise Him.

GERARD MANLEY HOPKINS.

Marvel of Marvels

Marvel of marvels, if I myself shall behold
With mine own eyes my King in His city of gold;
Where the least of lambs is spotless white in the fold,
Where the least and last of saints in spotless white is stoled,
Where the dimmest head beyond a moon is aureoled.
O saints, my belovèd, now mouldering to mould in the mould,
Shall I see you lift your heads, see your cerements unroll'd,
See with these very eyes? who now in darkness and cold
Tremble for the midnight cry, the rapture, the tale untold,—
The Bridegroom cometh, cometh, His Bride to enfold!

Cold it is, my belovèd, since your funeral bell was toll'd:
Cold it is, O my King, how cold alone on the wold!

CHRISTINA GEORGINA ROSSETTI.

Friends in Paradise

They are all gone into the world of light!
    And I alone sit lingering here;
Their very memory is fair and bright,
    And my sad thoughts doth clear :—

It glows and glitters in my cloudy breast,
    Like stars upon some gloomy grove,
Or those faint beams in which this hill is drest,
    After the sun's remove.

I see them walking in an air of glory,
    Whose light doth trample on my days:
My days, which are at best but dull and hoary,
    Mere glimmering and decays.

O holy Hope! and high Humility,
   High as the heavens above!
These are your walks, and you have shew'd them me.
    To kindle my cold love.

Dear, beauteous Death! the jewel of the just,
   Shining nowhere, but in the dark;
What mysteries do lie beyond thy dust,
    Could man outlook that mark!

He that hath found some fledged bird's nest, may know,
   At first sight, if the bird be flown;
But what fair well or grove he sings in now,
    That is to him unknown.

And yet, as Angels in some brighter dreams
   Call to the soul, when man doth sleep;
So some strange thoughts transcend our wonted themes,
    And into glory peep.
                   HENRY VAUGHAN.

Tree and Sky

Let my soul, a shining tree,
Silver branches lift towards thee,
Where on a hallowed winter's night
The clear-eyed angels may alight.

And if there should be tempests in
My spirit, let them surge like din
Of noble melodies at war;
With fervour of such blades of triumph as are
Flashed in white orisons of saints who go
On shafts of glory to the ecstasies they know.
                 SIEGFRIED SASSOON.

Matins

I cannot ope mine eyes,
But Thou art ready there to catch
My morning soul and sacrifice;
That we must needs for that day make a match.

My God, what is a heart?
Silver, or gold, or precious stone,
Or star, or rainbow, or a part
Of all these things, or all of them in one?

My God, what is a heart,
That Thou shouldst it so eye, and woo,
Pouring upon it all thy art,
As if that Thou hadst nothing else to do?

Indeed, man's whole estate
Amounts (and richly) to serve Thee:
He did not heav'n and earth create,
Yet studies them, not Him by whom they be.

Teach me Thy love to know;
That this new light which now I see,
May both the work and workman show;
Then by a sunbeam I will climb to Thee.

GEORGE HERBERT.

At a Solemn Music

Blest pair of Sirens, pledges of Heaven's joy,
Sphere-born harmonious Sisters, Voice and Verse!
Wed your divine sounds, and mixt power employ,
Dead things with inbreathed sense able to pierce;

And to our high-raised phantasy present
That undisturbéd Song of pure concent
Aye sung before the sapphire-colour'd throne
 To Him that sits thereon,
With saintly shout and solemn jubilee;
Where the bright Seraphim in burning row
Their loud uplifted angel-trumpets blow;
And the Cherubic host in thousand quires
Touch their immortal harps of golden wires,
With those just Spirits that wear victorious palms,
 Hymns devout and holy psalms
 Singing everlastingly:
That we on Earth, with undiscording voice
May rightly answer that melodious noise;
As once we did, till disproportion'd sin
Jarr'd against nature's chime, and with harsh din
Broke the fair music that all creatures made
To their great Lord, whose love their motion sway'd
In perfect diapason, whilst they stood
In first obedience, and their state of good.
O may we soon again renew that Song,
And keep in tune with Heaven, till God ere long
To his celestial consort us unite,
To live with Him, and sing in endless morn of light!
JOHN MILTON.

The Deluge

Though giant rains put out the sun,
 Here stand I for a sign.
Though Earth be filled with waters dark,
 My cup is filled with wine.
Tell to the trembling priests that here
 Under the deluge nod,
One nameless, tattered, broken man
 Stood up and drank to God.

Sun has been where the rain is now,
  Bees in the heat to hum,
Haply a humming maiden came,
  Now let the Deluge come:
Brown of aureole, green of garb,
  Straight as a golden rod,
Drink to the throne of thunder now!
  Drink to the wrath of God.

High in the wreck I held the cup,
  I clutched my rusty sword,
I cocked my tattered feather
  To the glory of the Lord.
Not undone were the heaven and earth,
  This hollow world thrown up,
Before one man had stood up straight,
  And drained it like a cup.
                    G. K. CHESTERTON.

From " The Song of Honour "

I heard it all, each, every note
Of every lung and tongue and throat,
Ay, every rhythm and rhyme
Of everything that lives and loves
And upward, ever upward moves
From lowly to sublime!
Earth's multitudinous Sons of Light,
I heard them lift their lyric might
With each and every charming sprite
That lit the sky that wondrous night
As far as eye could climb!

I heard it all, I heard the whole
Harmonious hymn of Being roll

Up through the chapel of my soul
And at the altar die,
And in the awful quiet then
Myself I heard, Amen, Amen,
Amen I heard me cry!
I heard it all and then although
I caught my flying senses, Oh,
A dizzy man was I!
I stood and stared; the sky was lit,
The sky was stars all over it,
I stood, I knew not why,
Without a wish, without a will,
I stood upon that silent hill
And stared into the sky until
My eyes were blind with stars, and still
I stared into the sky.

RALPH HODGSON.

From " Song to David "

Strong is the lion—like a coal
His eyeball,—like a bastion's mole
    His chest against the foes :
Strong the gier-eagle on his sail ;
Strong against the tide th' enormous whale
    Emerges as he goes.

But stronger still, in earth and air,
And in the sea, the man of prayer,
    And far beneath the tide :
And in the seat to faith assign'd,
Where ask is have, where seek is find,
    Where knock is open wide.

Precious the penitential tear;
And precious is the sigh sincere,
Acceptable to God:
And precious are the winning flowers,
In gladsome Israel's feast of bowers
Bound on the hallow'd sod.

Glorious the sun in mid career;
Glorious th' assembled fires appear;
Glorious the comet's train:
Glorious the trumpet and alarm;
Glorious the Almighty's stretch'd-out arm;
Glorious th' enraptured main:

Glorious the northern lights astream;
Glorious the song, when God's the theme;
Glorious the thunder's roar:
Glorious Hosanna from the den;
Glorious the catholic Amen;
Glorious the martyr's gore:

Glorious—more glorious—is the crown
of Him that brought salvation down,
By meekness call'd thy Son:
Thou that stupendous truth believed:—
And now the matchless deed's achieved,
Determined, dared, and done!

CHRISTOPHER SMART.

Revelation vii. 9–12

After these things I saw, and behold, a great multitude,
which no man could number, out of every nation, and of
all tribes and peoples and tongues, standing before the throne
and before the Lamb, arrayed in white robes, and palms in

their hands; and they cry with a great voice, saying, Salvation unto our God which sitteth on the throne, and unto the Lamb. And all the angels were standing round about the throne, and about the elders and the four living creatures; and they fell before the throne on their faces, and worshipped God, saying, Amen: Blessing, and glory, and wisdom, and thanksgiving, and honour, and power, and might, be unto our God for ever and ever. AMEN.

PART TWELVE

EXPECTATION

Producer:
F. FELTON.

Speakers:
FELIX AYLMER.
ROBERT HARRIS.
[*By kind permission of St. Martin's Theatre Management.*]
MARY GRAHAM.

Music:
Selected by F. FELTON.

" The Kingdom " (Elgar), Prelude.   H.M.V. DB1934.
" Clock " Symphony (Haydn), Adagio : Presto.
                                        Columbia L2088.
Symphony, No. 1, in C Minor (Brahms), 1st Movement.
                                        H.M.V. D1499.
Symphony, No. 1, in C Minor (Brahms), 4th Movement.
                                        H.M.V. D1502.

PROLOGUE

EXPECTATION is hope that makes no claim on the future. It awaits the event without seeking to shape it beforehand in its heart. It is in the pilgrim's journey the February hour, the hushed instant that trembles on the borders of spring. It is the moment of the seekers, the time before the swallow dares. So with shoulders braced, and swift limbs girt for action, the pilgrim leans forward knowing naught, guessing naught and certain of one thing only, that what's to come is still unsure, and, being unsure, matches the rising trouble in his blood.

What lies beyond? Man's estate for the child; and the second childhood that is the power, being old, to see with the child's eyes again. For one seeker the joy of the race, for another the scallop-shell of quiet, for a third Hellas reborn in the City of God at the other end of the road.

What change, what chance will come? The pilgrim does not ask. Sufficient that blossom is distantly beginning and that strange tidings are vocal in the air. He may, as he steps into the dawn, find it is news from outside time, of which he has heard the first earthly crying. He may be on his way to the coronation of the King of Kings. The pilgrim does not question. He is on the road, and to travel in expectation is at the road's first milestone better than to arrive.

Now Doth the Sun

Now doth the sun appear,
The mountains' snows decay
Crown'd with frail flowers forth comes the baby year.

My soul, time posts away;
And those yet in that frost
Which flower and fruit hath lost,
As if all here immortal were, dost stay.

For shame! thy powers awake.
Look to that heaven which never night makes black,
And there at that immortal sun's bright rage,
Deck thee with flowers which fear not rage of days.

WILLIAM DRUMMOND.

To Spring

O thou with dewy locks, who lookest down
Through the clear windows of the morning, turn
Thine angel eyes upon our western isle,
Which in full choir hails thy approach, O Spring!

The hills tell one another, and the listening
Valleys hear; all our longing eyes are turn'd
Up to thy bright pavilions: issue forth
And let thy holy feet visit our clime!

Come o'er the eastern hills, and let our winds
Kiss thy perfumèd garments; let us taste
Thy morn and evening breath; scatter thy pearls
Upon our lovesick land that mourns for thee.

O deck her forth with thy fair fingers; pour
Thy soft kisses on her bosom; and put
Thy golden crown upon her languish'd head,
When modest tresses are bound up for thee.

WILLIAM BLAKE.

Waiting Both

A star looks down at me,
And says: " Here I and you
Stand, each in our degree:
What do you mean to do?—
    Mean to do?"

I say: " For all I know
Wait, and let Time go by,
Till my change comes "—" Just so,"
The star says. " So mean I—
    So mean I."

THOMAS HARDY.

Times go by Turns

The toppèd tree in time may grow again.
Most naked plants renew both fruit and flower;
The soust wight may find release of pain,
The driest soil suck in some moist'ning shower,
Times go by turns and chances changed by course
From foul to fair, from better hap to worse.

The sea of fortune doth not ever flow.
She draws her favours to the lowest ebb;

Her time hath equal times to come and go,
Her loom doth weave the fine and coarsest web,
No joy so great but runneth to an end,
No hap so hard but may in fine amend.

Not always fall of leaf nor ever spring,
No endless night yet not eternal day;
The saddest birds a season find to sing,
The roughest storm, a calm may soon allay;
Thus with succeeding turns God tempereth all,
That man may hope to rise, yet fear to fall.

A chance may win that by mischance was lost;
The net that holds no great, takes little fish;
In some things all, in all things none are crost,
Few all they need, but none have all they wish;
Unmeddled joys have to no man befall;
Who least, hath some; who most, hath never all.

ROBERT SOUTHWELL.

The Seekers

Friends and loves we have none, nor wealth nor blessed abode,
But the hope of the City of God at the other end of the road.

Not for us are content, and quiet, and peace of mind,
For we go seeking a city that we shall never find.

There is no solace on earth for us—for such as we—
Who search for a hidden city that we shall never see.

Only the road and the dawn, the sun, the wind and the rain,
And the watch-fire under stars, and sleep, and the road again.

We travel the dusty road till the light of the day is dim,
And sunset shows us spires away on the world's rim.

We travel from dawn to dusk, till the day is past and by,
Seeking the Holy City beyond the rim of the sky.

Friends and loves we have none, nor wealth nor blest abode,
But the hope of the City of God at the other end of the road.

JOHN MASEFIELD.

The Song of the Ungirt Runners

We swing ungirded hips,
    And lightened are our eyes;
The rain is on our lips,
    We do not run for prize.
We know not whom we trust
    Nor whitherward we fare.
But we run because we must
    Through the great wide air.

The waters of the seas
    Are troubled as by storm.
The tempest strips the trees
    And does not leave them warm.
Does the tearing tempest pause?
    Do the tree-tops ask it why?
So we run without a care
    'Neath the big bare sky.

The rain is on our lips,
    We do not run for prize,
But the storm the water whips
    And the wave howls to the skies.

The winds arise and strike it
  And scatter it like the sand,
And we run because we like it
  Through the broad bright land.

CHARLES HAMILTON SORLEY.

Chartless

I never saw a moor,
I never saw the sea,
Yet now I know how the heather looks,
And what a wave must be.

I never spoke with God,
Nor visited in Heaven;
Yet certain am I of the spot
As if the chart were given.

EMILY DICKINSON.

A Second Childhood

When all my days are ending
And I have no song to sing,
I think I shall not be too old
To stare at everything;
As I stared once at a nursery door
Or a tall tree and a swing.

Wherein God's ponderous mercy hangs
On all my sins and me,
Because He does not take away
The terror from the tree
And stones still shine along the road
That are and cannot be.

Men grow too old for love, my love,
Men grow too old for wine,
But I shall not grow too old to see
Unearthly daylight shine,
Changing my chamber's dust to snow
Till I doubt if it be mine.

Behold, the crowning mercies melt,
The first surprises stay;
And in my dross is dropped a gift
For which I dare not pray:
That a man grow used to grief and joy
But not to night and day.

Men grow too old for love, my love,
Men grow too old for lies;
But I shall not grow too old to see
Enormous night arise,
A cloud that is larger than the world
And a monster made of eyes.

Nor am I worthy to unloose
The latchet of my shoe,
Or shake the dust from off my feet
Or the staff that bears me through
On ground that is too good to last,
Too solid to be true.

Men grow too old to woo, my love,
Men grow too old to wed:
But I shall not grow too old to see
Hung crazily overhead
Incredible rafters when I wake
And find I am not dead.

G. K. CHESTERTON.

Fleet Street

I never see the newsboys run
  Amid the whirling street,
  With swift untiring feet,
To cry the latest venture done,
But I expect one day to hear
  Them cry the crack of doom
  And risings from the tomb,
With great Archangel Michael near;
And see them running from the Fleet
  As messengers of God,
  With Heaven's tidings shod
About their brave unwearied feet.

SHANE LESLIE.

St. Luke xxi. 25–28

And there shall be signs in sun and moon and stars; and upon the earth distress of nations, in perplexity for the roaring of the sea and the billows;

Men fainting for fear, and for expectation of the things which are coming on the world: for the powers of the heavens shall be shaken.

And then shall they see the Son of Man coming in a cloud with power and great glory.

But when these things begin to come to pass, look up, and lift your heads; because your redemption draweth nigh.

PART THIRTEEN

CONTRITION

Producer:

F. Felton.

Speakers:

Robert Harris.

[*By kind permission of Alec Rea, Moss Empires and Howard Wyndham Tours Ltd.*]

Ion Swinley.

Music:

Selected by F. Felton.

Unfinished Symphony, in B Minor (Schubert), 1st Movement.   H.M.V. C1294.

Unfinished Symphony, in B Minor (Schubert), 1st and 2nd Movements.   H.M.V. C1295.

"The Kingdom" (Elgar), Prelude.   H.M.V. DB1934.

Trio, No. 7, in B Flat Major, Op. 97 (Beethoven), 3rd Movement.   H.M.V. D.B.1225.

Hammerklavier Sonata (Beethoven, *arr.* Weingartner), 2nd and 3rd Movements.   Columbia LX44.

PROLOGUE

" We have erred and strayed from Thy ways like lost sheep," murmurs the pilgrim at the City Gate. But under a storm of palms One rides past on the shepherd's mission, to fold His flock. . . .

So let the pilgrim be not ashamed of his contrite heart, whether the sorrow be of earth or beyond the world. Let him face his conscience with the vow that he will so live as not to fear its judgment. And if the son fears he is unworthy of his mother's gift of life or if the father laments his uncomforted child, let both believe that there wait pardon and understanding beyond the world. So that they need not fear the Might-have-been whose other names are No-more, Too-late, Farewell.

Then is there the contrition of the soul that has failed—as all must—of God, that bids Him to see his sin only through tears. Yet he need not despair of forgiveness while the blackbird whistles at the Gate for all the fallen, " Let her in. Let her in," and love, outsinging the blackbird, cries, " You must sit down and taste my meat." The manna from heaven is still spread on the tables of all the world.

The Maid's Lament

I Loved him not; and yet now he is gone
    I feel I am alone.
I check'd him while he spoke; yet, could he speak,
    Alas! I would not check.
For reasons not to love him once I sought,
    And wearied all my thought
To vex myself and him; I now would give
    My love, could he but live
Who lately lived for me, and when he found
    'Twas vain, in holy ground
He hid his face amid the shades of death.
    I waste for him my breath
Who wasted his for me; but mine returns,
    And this lorn bosom burns,
With stifling heat, heaving it up in sleep,
    And waking me to weep
Tears that had melted his soft heart: for years
    Wept he as bitter tears.
" Merciful God! " such was his latest prayer,
    " These may she never share! "
Quieter in his breath, his breast more cold
    Than daisies in the mould,
Where children spell, athwart the churchyard gate,
    His name and life's brief date.
Pray for him, gentle souls, whoe'er you be,
    And, O, pray too for me!

WALTER SAVAGE LANDOR.

To His Mother, C.L.M.

In the dark womb where I began
My mother's life made me a man.
Through all the months of human birth
Her beauty fed my common earth.

182

I cannot see, nor breathe, nor stir,
But through the death of some of her.

Down in the darkness of the grave
She cannot see the life she gave.
For all her love, she cannot tell
Whether I use it ill or well,
Nor knock at dusty doors to find
Her beauty dusty in the mind.

If the grave's gates could be undone,
She would not know her little son,
I am so grown.   If we should meet,
She would pass by me in the street,
Unless my soul's face let her see
My sense of what she did for me.

What have I done to keep in mind
My debt to her and womankind?
What woman's happier life repays
Her for those months of wretched days?
For all my mouthless body leech'd
Ere Birth's releasing hell was reach'd?

What have I done, or tried, or said
In thanks to that dear woman dead?
Men triumph over women still,
Men trample women's rights at will,
And man's lust roves the world untamed.

.   .   .   .   .

O grave, keep shut lest I be shamed.

JOHN MASEFIELD.

The Toys

My little Son, who look'd from thoughtful
    eyes,
And moved and spoke in quiet grown-up
    wise,
Having my law the seventh time disobey'd,
I struck him, and dismiss'd
With hard words and unkiss'd,
His Mother, who was patient, being dead.
Then, fearing lest his grief should hinder
    sleep,
I visited his bed,
But found him slumbering deep,
With darken'd eyelids, and their lashes yet
From his late sobbing wet.
And I, with moan,
Kissing away his tears, left others of my
    own;
For, on a table drawn beside his head,
He had put, within his reach,
A box of counters and a red-vein'd stone,
A piece of glass abraded by the beach,
And six or seven shells,
A bottle with bluebells,
And two French copper coins, ranged there
    with careful art,
To comfort his sad heart.
So when that night I pray'd
To God, I wept, and said:
Ah! when at last we lie with tranced breath,
Not vexing Thee in death,
And Thou rememberest of what toys
We made our joys,
How weakly understood
Thy great commanded good,

184

Then fatherly not less
Than I whom Thou hast moulded from the clay,
Thou'lt leave Thy wrath, and say,
" I will be sorry for their childishness."

COVENTRY PATMORE.

A Superscription

Look in my face; my name is Might-have-been;
  I am also called No-more, Too-late, Farewell;
  Unto thine ear I hold the dead-sea shell
Cast up thy Life's foam-fretted feet between;
Unto thine eyes the glass where that is seen
  Which had Life's form and Love's, but by my spell
  Is now a shaken shadow intolerable,
Of ultimate things unuttered the frail screen.

Mark me, how still I am! But should there dart
  One moment through thy soul the soft surprise
  Of that winged Peace which lulls the breath of sighs,—
Then shalt thou see me smile, and turn apart
Thy visage to mine ambush at thy heart
  Sleepless with cold commemorative eyes.

DANTE GABRIEL ROSSETTI.

Anguish

My God and King! to Thee
  I bow my knee;
I bow my troubled soul, and greet
With my foul heart thy holy feet.
Cast it, or tread it! it shall do
Even what thou wilt, and praise thee too.

185

My God, could I weep blood,
　Gladly I would,
Or if thou wilt give me that art,
Which through the eyes pours out the heart,
I will exhaust it all, and make
Myself all tears, a weeping lake.

O! 'tis an easy thing
　To write and sing;
But to write true, unfeigned verse
Is very hard! O God, disperse
These weights, and give my spirit leave
To act as well as to conceive!

O my God, hear my cry;
　Or let me die! . . .

HENRY VAUGHAN.

2 *Samuel* xii.

And the Lord sent Nathan unto David. And he came unto him, and said unto him, There were two men in one city; the one rich, and the other poor. The rich man had exceeding many flocks and herds: but the poor man had nothing, save one little ewe lamb, which he had bought and nourished up: and it grew up together with him, and with his children; it did eat of his own morsel, and drank of his own cup, and lay in his bosom, and was unto him as a daughter.

And there came a traveller unto the rich man, and he spared to take of his own flock and of his own herd, to dress for the wayfaring man that was come unto him, but took the poor man's lamb, and dressed it for the man that was come to him.

And David's anger was greatly kindled against the man; and he said to Nathan, As the Lord liveth, the man that hath done this is worthy to die: And he shall restore the lamb fourfold, because he did this thing, and because he had no pity.

And Nathan said to David, Thou art the man. Wherefore hast thou despised the word of the Lord, to do that which is evil in his sight? Thou hast smitten Uriah the Hittite with the sword, and hast taken his wife to be thy wife, and has slain him with the sword of the children of Ammon.

And David said unto Nathan, I have sinned against the Lord. And Nathan said unto David, the Lord also hath put away thy sin; thou shalt not die.

A Litany

Drop, drop, slow tears,
   And bathe those beauteous feet
Which brought from Heaven
   The news and Prince of Peace:
Cease not, wet eyes,
   His mercy to entreat;
To cry for vengeance
   Sin doth never cease.
In your deep floods
   Drown all my faults and fears;
Nor let His eye
   See sin, but through my tears.

PHINEAS FLETCHER.

Prayer to the Virgin

(A paraphrase of François Villon's prayer for his mother)

Queen of the Earth, and Lady of the Sky,
Empress of Heaven and the dark pit of Hell,
Give ear unto a humble Christian's cry
That she may come to thee in Heaven to dwell.

My sins weigh on me—more than tongue can tell;
But merciful art thou, and thy grace all free.
Without thy grace I cannot come to thee,
Without thy help no soul may win the Sky;
Sincere I kneel; look down and pity me,
For in this faith I wish to live and die.

I am a poor old woman, shrunk and lean;
Nothing I know, I cannot read or spell.
Yet painted in the cloister I have seen
Thy lute-filled mansions o'er the deeps of Hell
Where the damned roll down in fire perpetual.
I tremble; then I hope. Have pity on me!
Lady of Grace, I put all trust in thee;
And lifting hands unto thy throne on high
Invoke thee of thy Love and deep Pitie,
For in this faith I wish to live and die.

HERBERT PALMER.

Love

Love bade me welcome; yet my soul drew back,
 Guilty of dust and sin.
But quick-eyed Love, observing me grow slack
 From my first entrance in,
Drew nearer to me, sweetly questioning
 If I lacked anything.

" A guest," I answer'd, " worthy to be here ":
 Love said, " You shall be he."
" I, the unkind, ungrateful? Ah, my dear,
 I cannot look on Thee."
Love took my hand and smiling did reply,
 " Who made the eyes but I? "

" Truth, Lord ; but I have marr'd them ; let my shame
    Go where it doth deserve."
" And know you not," says Love, " Who bore the blame ?"
    " My dear, then I will serve."
" You must sit down," says Love, " and taste my meat."
    So I did sit and eat.

GEORGE HERBERT.

PART FOURTEEN

ASSURANCE

Producer:

Miss B. BURNHAM.

Speakers:

NESTA SAWYER.
ROBERT SPEAIGHT.
ION SWINLEY.

Music:

Selected by Miss B. BURNHAM.

Symphony, No. 41, in C Major (Mozart), 1st Movement.   Columbia LX282.

Symphony, No. 41, in C Major (Mozart), 2nd Movement.   Columbia LX283.

Quintet in A Major (Mozart), 2nd Movement.
                                Columbia L2253.

PROLOGUE

ASSURANCE is the knowledge of power. Hours of dark and doubt are many, and through their many spells we have walked by the pilgrim, when his feet were almost gone. But there are high and compensating moments. In one such a moment the pilgrim sets the trumpet to his lips and sounds the great glory of strife. That is power—to be assured that there is the struggle and that it avails. Not less in the quiet of the poised spirit is there the strength of virtue, which seals its own with a triple armour. There is the unassailable vitality that dwells with wise innocence, and brightens the vision of the eye untarnished.

These are great allies for the pilgrim. As great or greater still are the certainties of love, whose sentinels ring out " all's well " in the space between a star and a star. This is the love of earth. Surpassing even the love of women is the revealed love of the divine lover. To that espousal the pilgrim moves on light unfaltering foot. Little need he care for the hostilities of Time. He can outrun that leaden gaoler. Yes and outpace one darker still. Death is a short step from a lesser into a greater light. His pride is defeated. Death dies of his own mortality. Death shall die, and in life, for ever set free of his black neighbourhood, at the height of Assurance, as at its source, the pilgrim sees his Lord face to face in the truth of everlasting day.

Answer

Sound, sound the clarion, fill the fife!
To all the sensual world proclaim,
One crowded hour of glorious life
Is worth an age without a name.

WALTER SCOTT.

Integer Vitae

The man of life upright,
  Whose guiltless heart is free
From all dishonest deeds
  Or thought of vanity;

The man whose silent days
  In harmless joys are spent,
Whom hopes cannot delude,
  Nor sorrow discontent:

That man needs neither towers
  Nor armour for defence.
Nor secret vaults to fly
  From thunder's violence:

He only can behold
  With unaffrighted eyes
The horrors of the deep
  And terrors of the skies.

Thus, scorning all the cares
  That fate or fortune brings,
He makes the heaven his book,
  His wisdom heavenly things:

194

Good thoughts his only friends.
His wealth a well-spent age,
The earth his sober inn,
And quiet pilgrimage.

THOMAS CAMPION.

From " Auguries of Innocence "

To see a World in a grain of sand,
And a heaven in a wild flower,
Hold Infinity in the palm of your hand,
And Eternity in an hour. . . .

The bat that flits at close of eve
Has left the brain that won't believe.
The owl that calls upon the night
Speaks the unbeliever's fright. . . .

Joy and woe are woven fine,
A clothing for the soul divine;
Under every grief and pine
Runs a joy with silken twine. . . .

Every tear from every eye
Becomes a babe in Eternity. . . .

The bleat, the bark, bellow, and roar
Are waves that beat on Heaven's shore. . . .

He who doubts from what he sees
Will ne'er believe, do what you please.
If the Sun and Moon should doubt,
They'd immediately go out. . . .

WILLIAM BLAKE.

Sonnet cxvi.

Let me not to the marriage of true minds
Admit impediments. Love is not love
Which alters when it alteration finds,
Or bends with the remover to remove:
O, no! it is an ever-fixèd mark,
That looks on tempests and is never shaken;
It is the star to every wand'ring bark,
Whose worth's unknown, although his height be taken.
Love's not Time's fool, though rosy lips and cheeks
Within his bending sickle's compass come:
Love alters not with his brief hours and weeks,
But bears it out even to the edge of doom :—
 If this be error and upon me proved,
 I never writ, nor no man ever loved.

WILLIAM SHAKESPEARE.

From " In Memoriam "

No longer half-akin to brute,
 For all we thought and loved and did,
 And hoped, and suffer'd, is but seed
Of what in them is flower and fruit;

Whereof the man, that with me trod
 This planet, was a noble type
 Appearing ere the times were ripe,
That friend of mine who lives in God,

That God, which ever lives and loves,
 One God, one law, one element,
 And one far-off divine event,
To which the whole creation moves.

TENNYSON.

*From " A Hymn to the Name and Honour of
the admirable Saint Teresa "*

Angels, thy old friends, there shall greet thee
Glad at their own home now to meet thee.
All thy good works which went before,
And waited for thee at the door,
Shall own thee there; and all in one
Wear a constellation
Of crowns, with which the King, thy Spouse,
Shall build up thy triumphant brows,
All thy old woes shall now smile on thee,
And thy pains sit bright upon thee.
All thy sorrows here shall shine,
And thy sufferings be divine.
Tears shall take comfort, and turn gems,
And wrongs repent to diadems.
Even thy deaths shall live, and new
Dress the soul that erst they slew.

RICHARD CRASHAW.

From " My Beloved is Mine "

Ev'n like two little bank-dividing brooks,
  That wash the pebbles with their wanton streams,
And having ranged and search'd a thousand nooks,
  Meet both at length in silver-breasted Thames,
  Where in a greater current they conjoin
So I my Best-Beloved's am, so He is mine.

Ev'n so we met; and after long pursuit
  Ev'n so we joined; we both became entire;
No need for either to renew a suit,
  For I was flax and He was flames of fire:
  Our firm-united souls did more than twine;
So I my Best-Beloved's am, so He is mine.

If all those glittering Monarchs that command
   The servile quarters of this earthly ball,
Should tender in exchange their shares of land,
   I would not change my fortunes for them all :
   Their wealth is but a counter to my coin ;
The world's but theirs : but my Beloved's mine.

FRANCIS QUARLES.

On Time

Fly envious Time, till thou run out thy race,
Call on the lazy leaden-stepping hours,
Whose speed is but the heavy Plummets pace ;
And glut thyself with what thy womb devours,
Which is no more than what is false and vain
And merely mortal dross ;
So little is our loss,
So little is thy gain.
For when as each thing bad thou hast entomb'd,
And last of all, thy greedy self consum'd,
Then long eternity shall greet our bliss
With an individual kiss ;
And Joy shall overtake us as a flood,
When everything that is sincerely good
And perfectly divine,
With Truth, and Peace, and Love shall ever shine
About the supreme Throne
Of him, t'whose happy-making sight alone
When once our heavenly-guided soul shall climb
Then all this earthy grossness quit,
Attired with stars, we shall for ever sit,
Triumphing over Death, and Chance, and thee, O
   Time.

JOHN MILTON.

Prospice

Fear death?—to feel the fog in my throat,
    The mist in my face,
When the snows begin, and the blasts denote
    I am nearing the place,
The power of the night, the press of the storm,
    The post of the foe;
Where he stands, the Arch Fear in a visible form,
    Yet the strong man must go:
For the journey is done and the summit attained,
    And the barriers fall,
Though a battle's to fight ere the guerdon be gained,
    The reward of it all.
I was ever a fighter, so—one fight more,
    The best and the last!
I would hate that death bandaged my eyes, and forbore,
    And bade me creep past.
No! let me taste the whole of it, fare like my peers
    The heroes of old,
Bear the brunt, in a minute pay glad life's arrears
    Of pain, darkness and cold.
For sudden the worst turns the best to the brave,
    The black minute's at end,
And the elements rage, the fiend-voices that rave,
    Shall dwindle, shall blend,
Shall change, shall become first a peace out of pain,
    Then a light, then thy breast,
O thou soul of my soul! I shall clasp thee again,
    And with God be the rest!

ROBERT BROWNING.

Death

Death, be not proud, though some have callèd thee
   Mighty and dreadful, for thou art not so:
   For those whom thou think'st thou dost overthrow
Die not, poor death; not yet canst thou kill me.
From rest and sleep, which but thy pictures be,
   Much pleasure, then from thee much more must
      flow;
   And soonest our best men with thee do go—
Rest of their bones and souls' delivery!
Thou'rt slave to fate, chance, kings and desperate
      men,
   And dost with poison, war, and sickness dwell;
   And poppy or charms can make us sleep as well
And better than thy stroke. Why swell'st thou
      then?
   One short sleep past, we wake eternally,
And Death shall be no more: Death thou shalt
      die.

JOHN DONNE.

From " The Dream of Gerontius "

Take me away, and in the lowest deep
   There let me be,
And there in hope the lone night-watches keep,
   Told out for me.
There, motionless and happy in my pain,
   Lone, not forlorn—
There will I sing my sad perpetual strain,
   Until the morn,
There will I sing, and soothe my stricken breast,
   Which ne'er can cease

To throb, and pine, and languish, till possest
    Of its Sole Peace.
There will I sing my absent Lord and Love :—
    Take me away,
That sooner I may rise, and go above,
And see Him in the truth of everlasting day.

JOHN HENRY NEWMAN.

PART FIFTEEN

REVERENCE

Producer:

Miss M. H. ALLEN.

Speakers:

ROBERT SPEAIGHT.

DENNIS ARUNDELL.

Music:

Selected by MAURICE BROWN.

Symphony, No. 9, in D Minor (Beethoven), 2nd and 3rd
    Movements.   H.M.V. DB2330.

Symphony, No. 9, in D Minor (Beethoven), 3rd Move-
    ment.   H.M.V. DB2331.

Symphony, No. 9, in D Minor (Beethoven), 3rd and 4th
    Movements.   H.M.V. DB2332.

PROLOGUE

REVERENCE is the recognition of the better by the good. The pilgrim, knowing both the weakness and the strength of his own heart, looks beyond to where weakness is cancelled and strength intensified is made one thing with loveliness.

On all hands, if he will but look, these astonishments await his approach. It may be that awe visits him in the presence of man's creative glory. The voice of Homer may remind him of the conquest of time by man's eternal vision. Or under his feet in the loving filigree of the snowflake he may detect the absolute achievement of the greatest craftsman of all.

There is reverence for human striving to perfection, but in its pure form that emotion is reserved for the neighbourhood of God. Love is of the essence here—love which in its intense perception surpasses the slower victories of reason. This tender love finds its object everywhere—on the marshes, among the beasts in the field and in the untrodden spaces of the stars. It leans out and onward, daring even to envisage immortality through the many-coloured dome of glass. But in its simplicity this love knows that, only when the colours, redeemed by suffering, put on the flawless white, will the pilgrim see face to face the Living One—who is the perfectible image of all man's desire.

On first looking in Chapman's Homer

Much have I travelled in the realms of gold,
   And many goodly states and kingdoms seen :
   Round many western islands have I been
Which bards in fealty to Apollo hold.
Oft of one wide expanse had I been told
   That deep-browed Homer ruled as his demesne,
   Yet never did I breathe its pure serene
Till I heard Chapman speak out loud and bold ;
Then felt I like some watcher of the skies
   When a new planet swims into his ken ;
Or like stout Cortez when with eagle eyes
   He stared at the Pacific—and all his men
Looked at each other with a wild surmise—
   Silent, upon a peak in Darien.

JOHN KEATS.

To a Snowflake

What heart could have thought you ?—
Past our devisal
(O *filigree petal* !)
Fashioned so purely
Fragilely, surely,
From what Paradisal
Imagineless metal
Too costly for cost ?
What hammered you, wrought you,
From Argentine vapour ?—

God was my shaper.
Passing survival.
He hammered, He wrought me,
From curled silver vapor,
To lust of his mind ;—

206

Thou couldst not have thought me!
So purely, so palely,
Timely, surely,
Mightily, frailly,
Insculped and embossed,
With His hammer of wind,
And His graver of frost.

FRANCIS THOMPSON.

Helen

Helen, thy beauty is to me
  Like those Nicaean basks of yore,
That gently, o'er a perfumed sea,
  The weary, wayworn wanderer bore
  To his own native shore.

On desperate seas long wont to roam
  Thy hyacinth hair, thy classic face,
Thy Naiad airs have brought me home
  To the glory that was Greece
  And the grandeur that was Rome.

Lo! in your brilliant window-niche
  How statue-like I see thee stand,
The agate-lamp within thy hand!
  Ah, Psyche, from the regions which
  Are Holy Land.

EDGAR ALLAN POE.

Draw in thy Beams

Leave me, O Love, which reachest but to dust!
And thou, my mind, aspire to higher things!
Grow rich in that which never taketh rust;
Whatever fades but fading pleasure brings.

Draw in thy beams, and humble all thy might
To that sweet yoke where lasting freedoms be,
Which breaks the clouds and opens forth the light
That doth both shine and give us sight to see.
O take fast hold! Let that light be thy guide
In this small course which birth draws out to death,
And think how evil becometh him to slide
Who seeketh Heaven, and comes of heavenly breath!
Then farewell, World! Thy uttermost I see,
Eternal Love, maintain thy love in me.

SIR PHILIP SIDNEY.

The Dawning

Yet let my course, my aim, my love,
And chief acquaintance be above.
So when that day and hour shall come,
On which Thy Self will be the sun,
Thou'lt find me dressed and on my way,
Watching the break of Thy great day.

HENRY VAUGHAN.

Marshes of Glynn

As the marsh-hen secretly builds on the watery sod,
Behold I will build me a nest on the greatness of God;
I will fly in the greatness of God, as the marsh-hen flies,
In the freedom that fills all the space 'twixt the marsh
     and the skies.

By so many roots as the marsh-grass sends in the sod,
I will heartily lay me ahold on the greatness of God:
O, like to the greatness of God is the greatness within
The range of the marshes, the liberal marshes of Glynn.

SIDNEY LANIER.

To his ever-loving God

Can I not come to thee, my God, for these
so very many meeting hindrances,
That slack my pace, but yet not make me stay?
Who slowly goes, rids, in the end, his way.
Cleere thou my paths, or shorten thou my miles,
Remove the barrs, or lift me o'er the stiles;
Since rough the way is, help me when I call,
And take me up, or else prevent the fall.
I kenn my home, and it affords some ease
To see far off the smoking villages.
Fain would I rest, yet covet not to die,
For feare of future biting penurie;
No, no, my God thou know'st my wishes be
To leave this life, not loving it, but Thee.

ROBERT HERRICK.

Christ in the Universe

No planet knows that this
Our wayside planet, carrying land and wave,
Love and life multiplied, and pain and bliss
Bears, as chief treasure, one forsaken grave.
Nor, in our little day,
May his devices with the heavens be guessed,
His pilgrimage to thread the Milky Way,
Or His bestowals there be manifest.
But in the eternities,
Doubtless we shall compare together, hear
A million alien Gospels, in what guise
He trod the Pleiades, the Lyre, the Bear

O, be prepared, my soul!
To read the inconceivable, to scan,
The million forms of God those stars unroll,
When, in our turn, we show to them a Man.

ALICE MEYNELL.

The Implicit Promise of Immortality

For some, methinks, in no less noble wise
Divine prevision kindles in the eyes,
When all have thoughts like frighted harpies flown
In her own beauty leave the soul alone;
When love—not rosy—flushed as he began,
But Love, still Love, the prisoned God in man—
Shows his face glorious, shakes his banner free,
Cries like a captain for eternity!
O halcyon air across the storms of youth,
O trust him, he is true, he is one with truth!
Nay, is he Christ? I know not; no man knows.
The right name of the heavenly Anteros—
But here is God, whatever God may be,
And whomso'er we worship, this is he.

F. W. H. MYERS.

An Hymn of Heavenly Love

Yet, O most blessed Spirit! Pure lamp of light,
Eternal spring of grace and wisdom true!
Vouchsafe to shed into my barren sprite
Some little drop of thy celestial dew,
That may my rhymes with sweet infuse embrew,
    And give me words equal unto my thought,
    To tell the marvels by thy mercy wrought!

Yet being pregnant still with powerful grace,
And full of fruitful love, that loves to get
Things like himself, and to enlarge his race,
His second brood, though not in power so great
Yet full of beauty, next he did beget,
    And infinite increase of Angels bright
    All glistening glorious in their Maker's sight.

To them the heaven's illimitable height
(Not this round heaven, which we from hence behold,
Adorned with thousand lamps of burning light,
And with ten thousand gems of shining gold)
He gave as their inheritance to hold
    That they might serve him in eternal bliss
    And be partakers of those joys of his.

EDMUND SPENSER.

Christ Crucified

Thy restless feet now cannot go
    For us and our eternal good,
As they were ever wont. What though
    They swim, alas! in their own flood?

Thy hands to give Thou canst not lift,
    Yet will Thy hand still giving be;
It gives, but O, itself's the gift!
    It gives tho' bound, tho' bound 'tis free!

RICHARD CRASHAW.

Revelation i. 10, 12–18

I was in the Spirit on the Lord's day, and I heard behind me a great voice, as of a trumpet. And I turned to see the voice which spake with me. And having turned I saw seven golden candlesticks one like unto a son of man clothed with a garment down to the foot, and girt about at the breasts with a golden girdle. And his head and his hair were white as white wool, white as snow; and his eyes were as a flame of fire; and his feet like unto burnished brass, as if it had been refined in a furnace; and his voice as the voice of many waters. And he had in his hand seven stars: and out of his mouth proceeded a sharp two-edged sword: and his countenance was as the sun shineth in his strength. And when I saw him, I fell at his feet as one dead. And he laid his right hand upon me, saying, Fear not; I am the first and the last and the Living One; and I was dead, and behold, I am alive for evermore, and I have the keys of death and of Hades.

PART SIXTEEN

ECSTASY

Producer:

F. FELTON.

Speakers:

ROBERT SPEAIGHT.

ION SWINLEY

Music:

Selected by F. FELTON.

" The Kingdom " (Elgar), Prelude.   H.M.V. DB1934.

" Eventyr " (Delius).   Columbia SDX5.

" A Song before Sunrise " (Delius).   H.M.V. D1697.

Concerto, No. 2, in C Minor (Rachmaninoff), 1st and 2nd Movements.   H.M.V. DB1334.

Concerto, No. 2, in C Minor (Rachmaninoff), 2nd and 3rd Movements.   H.M.V. DB1336.

" Háry Janos," Suite (Zoltan Kodaly).   H.M.V. DB2458.

" Eventyr " (Delius).

Columbia SDX4 and Columbia SDX5.

PROLOGUE

THIS is the instant of release. Burdens have become wings and the spirit beats up to poise over time like a hawk, approaching the source of light as though drawn upward with the dews.

Though the end of the ascent is the same, there are many stairways in the house of heaven. But no pilgrim will dare the adventure of height without the single spark, whose bright ignition starts the wings on their sweep out and on. There is the way of travel—either in time or space, or out of both. To rise with the lark, to tumble with the eagle, to return to one's loved youth, to peer over the edge of the world, these are all one way. Another and more certain is by the liberties of love—the love whether of women or of disembodied loveliness. As surely is the freedom given to the soul by the awakening into love as by the vision of earthly beauty flowering into its heavenly counterpart.

There follows the absolute ecstasy of the shaken mind tragically free for ever of its shackles, commanding the world with its furious fancies. But beyond these troubles is the region of soul and rapt contemplation in perfect equipoise. Here ecstasy returns upon itself, like light upon its reflection. The air is not merely lit but fragrant with that white and single flame.

Invocation

O wanderer into many brains,
  O spark the emperor's purple hides,
You sow the dusk with fiery grains
When the gold horseman rides.
  O beauty on the darkness hurled,
  Be it through me you shame the world.

JOHN MASEFIELD.

Oxford

I came to Oxford in the light
  Of a spring-coloured afternoon;
Some clouds were grey and some were white,
  And all were blown to such a tune
Of quiet rapture in the sky,
I laughed to see them laughing by.

I had been dreaming in the train
  With thoughts at random from my book;
I looked, and read, and looked again,
  And suddenly to greet my look
Oxford shone up with every tower
Aspiringly sweetly like a flower.

Home turn the feet of men that seek,
  And home the hearts of children turn,
And none can teach the hour to speak
  What every hour is free to learn;
And all discover, late or soon,
Their golden Oxford afternoon.

GERALD GOULD.

When I set out for Lyonnesse

When I set out for Lyonnesse,
  A hundred miles away,
  The rime was on the spray,
And starlight lit my lonesomeness
When I set out for Lyonnesse
  A hundred miles away.

What would bechance at Lyonnesse
  While I should sojourn there
  No prophet durst declare,
Nor did the wisest wizard guess
What would bechance at Lyonnesse
  While I should sojourn there.

When I came back from Lyonnesse
  With magic in my eyes,
  All marked with mute surmise
My radiance rare and fathomless,
When I came back from Lyonnesse
  With magic in my eyes!

                    THOMAS HARDY.

Awake, my Heart, to be Loved

Awake, my heart, to be loved, awake, awake!
The darkness silvers away, the morn doth break,
It leaps in the sky: unrisen lustres slake
The o'ertaken moon. Awake, O heart, awake!

She too that loveth awaketh and hopes for thee;
Her eyes already have sped the shades that flee,
Already they watch the path thy feet shall take:
Awake, O heart, to be loved, awake, awake!

217

And if thou tarry from her,—if this could be,—
She cometh herself, O heart, to be loved, to thee;
For thee would unashamed herself forsake:
Awake to be loved, my heart, awake, awake!

Awake, the land is scattered with light, and see,
Uncanopied sleep is flying from field and tree:
And blossoming boughs of April in laughter shake;
Awake, O heart, to be loved, awake, awake!

Lo, all things wake and tarry and look for thee:
She looketh and saith, " O sun, now bring him to me.
Come more adored, O adored, for his coming's sake,
And awake my heart to be loved: awake, awake! "

ROBERT BRIDGES.

Sonnets from the Portuguese, 5

When our two souls stand up erect and strong,
  Face to face, silent, drawing nigh and nigher,
  Until the lengthening wings break into fire
At either curving point,—what bitter wrong
Can the earth do us, that we should not long
  Be here contented? Think! In mounting higher,
  The angels would press on us, and aspire
To drop some golden orb of perfect song
Into our deep dear silence. Let us stay
  Rather on earth, Belovèd—where the unfit
Contrarious moods of men recoil away
  And isolate pure spirits, and permit
A place to stand and love in for a day,
  With darkness and the death-hour rounding it.

ELIZABETH BARRETT BROWNING.

218

From " The Old Ships "

But I have seen
Pointing her shapely shadows from the dawn
And image tumbled on a rose-swept bay
A drowsy ship of some yet older day ;
And, wonder's breath indrawn,
Thought I—who knows—who knows—but in that same
(Fished up beyond Æææa, patched up new
—Stern painted brighter blue—)
That talkative, bald-headed seaman came
(Twelve patient comrades sweating at the oar)
From Troy's doom-crimson shore,
And with great lies about his wooden horse
Set the crew laughing, and forgot his course.

It was so old a ship—who knows, who knows?
—And yet so beautiful, I watched in vain
To see the mast burst open with a rose,
And the whole deck put on its leaves again.

JAMES ELROY FLECKER.

Wisdom

When Wisdom tells me that the world's a speck
Lost on the shoreless blue of God's To-Day. . . .
I smile and think, " For every man his way :
The world's my ship, and I'm alone on deck ! "

And when he tells me that the world's a spark
Lit in the whistling gloom of God's To-Night. . . .
I look within me to the edge of dark,
And dream, " The world's my field, and I'm the lark,
Alone with upward song, alone with light ! "

SIEGFRIED SASSOON.

Tom O'Bedlam

The moon's my constant mistress,
    And the lovely owl my marrow;
        The flaming drake,
        And the night-crow, make
Me music to my sorrow.

I know more than Apollo;
    For oft, when he lies sleeping,
        I behold the stars
        At mortal wars,
And the rounded welkin weeping.

The moon embraces her shepherd,
    And the Queen of Love her warrior;
        While the first does horn
        The stars of the morn,
And the next the heavenly farrier.

With a heart of furious fancies,
    Whereof I am commander:
        With a burning spear,
        And a horse of air,
To the wilderness I wander:

With a knight of ghosts and shadows,
    I summoned am to Tourney:
        Ten leagues beyond
        The wide world's end;
Methinks it is no journey.

ANONYMOUS.

The Donkey

When fishes flew and forests walked
    And figs grew upon thorn,
Some moment when the moon was blood
    Then surely I was born.

With monstrous head and sickening cry
    And ears like errant wings,
The devil's walking parody
    On all four-footed things.

The tattered outlaw of the earth,
    Of ancient crooked will;
Starve, scourge, deride me: I am dumb,
    I keep my secret still.

Fools! For I also had my hour;
    One far fierce hour and sweet:
There was a shout about my ears,
    And palms before my feet.

                G. K. CHESTERTON.

The Starlight Night

Look at the stars! Look, look up at the skies!
  O look at all the firefolk sitting there!
  The bright boroughs, the quivering citadels there!
The dim woods quick with diamond-wells! The elf-eyes!
The grey lawns cold where quaking gold-dew lies!
  Wind-beat whitebeam! Airy abeles all on flare!
  Flake-doves sent floating out at a farmyard scare!—
Ah, well! It is a purchase and a prize.

Buy then! Bid then!—What?—Prayer, patience, alms, vows—
Look, look! A May-mess, like on orchard-boughs!
    Look! March-bloom, like on mealed-with-yellow sallows!
These are indeed the barn; within-doors house
The shocks. This piece-bright paling hides the Spouse,
    Christ, and the mother of Christ and all His hallows.

GERARD MANLEY HOPKINS.

Love

Immortal Love, author of this great frame,
    Sprung from that beauty which can never fade;
    How hath man parcelled out Thy glorious name,
And thrown it on that dust which Thou hast made.

While mortal love doth all the title gain!
    Which siding with invention, they together
    Bear all the sway, possessing heart and brain
(Thy workmanship), and give Thee share in neither.

Wit fancies beauty, beauty raiseth wit;
    The world is theirs; they two play out the game,
    Thou stand by: and though Thy glorious name
Wrought out deliverance from th' infernal pit,

    Who sings Thy praise? Only a scarf or glove
    Doth warm our hands, and make them write of love.

GEORGE HERBERT.

Easter Hymn

Death, and darkness get you packing,
Nothing now to man is lacking,
All your triumphs now are ended.
And what Adam marr'd is mended;

222

Graves are beds now for the weary,
Death a nap, to wake more merry;
Youth now, full of pious duty,
Seeks in thee for perfect beauty.
The weak, and aged tir'd, with length
of daies, from thee look for new strength,
And infants with thy pangs contest
As pleasant, as if with the brest;
Then, unto him, who thus hath thrown
Even to Contempt thy kingdom down,
And by his blood did us advance
Unto his own Inheritance,
To him be glory, power, praise
From this unto the last of daies.

HENRY VAUGHAN.

PART SEVENTEEN

PEACE

Producer :

F. FELTON.

Speakers :

ROBERT HARRIS.

ROBERT SPEAIGHT.

Music :

Selected by F. FELTON

" Blest are they that mourn " (Brahms), 1st Part.
                    H.M.V. C2382.

" Blest are they that mourn " (Brahms), 3rd Part.
                    H.M.V. C2383.

" Hassan " (Delius)   Columbia SDX7.

" Midsummer Night's Dream," Overture (Mendelssohn),
   2nd Part.   H.M.V. D1626.

Prelude, No. 8, " La fille aux cheveux de lin " (Debussy).
                    H.M.V. DA1243.

PROLOGUE

THE end of the Pilgrim's road is Peace. Far behind—so far
that its outline is dim as dream—glimmers the tranquil
country-side of youth. He has travelled far since then, and
has left much of his soul by the way. Here he stumbled in
the quicksand of ambition, there he was lost in the jungle
of passion; further still the fevers of despair shook and rent
him, and last of all the ultimate doubt both of self and of
the Creator. But the Pilgrim, who has endured and with-
stood, finds at the end of the road that the first tranquillity
of all returns ennobled and enriched with loss, with suffering
and with knowledge. He has heard a Voice whisper to him
in broken phrases as he has striven and fallen. Now those
unrelated sentences shape themselves, and grow together in a
healing unity. The Voice is soft as the beat of the Pilgrim's
heart, but clear as a bell ringing the bride home. "Peace,"
says the Voice, "Peace I leave with you; my peace I give
unto you."

The Princess

The stone-grey roses by the desert's rim,
Are soft-edged shadows on the moonlit sand,
Grey are the broken walls of Conchubar
That haunt of nightingales, whose voices are
Fountains that bubble in the dream-soft Moon.

Shall the Gazelles with moonbeam pale bright feet
Entering the vanished gardens sniff the air—
Some scent may linger of that ancient time,
Musician's song, or poet's passionate rhyme,
The Princess dead, still wandering love-sick there.

A Princess pale and cold as mountain snow,
In cool, dark chambers sheltered from the sun,
With long dark lashes and small delicate hands,
All Persia sighed to kiss her small, red mouth
Until they buried her in shifting sand.

And the Gazelles shall flit by in the Moon
And never shake the frail Tree's lightest leaves,
And moonlight roses perfume the pale Dawn
Until the scarlet life from her lips drawn
Gathers its shattered beauty in the sky.

WALTER J. TURNER.

Grey

Grey of the twilight, come,
Spread those wide wings above our meadows: bring
Coolness and mist: make dumb
The jarring noise of day; and gently ring

228

Our woods and ponds with dimness; take away
All busy stir, but let the grey owl sway
Noiselessly over the bough like a little ghost:
And let the cricket in the dark hedge sing
His withered note: and O Immortal Host,
Welcome this traveller to your drowsy hall
And, standing at the porch, speechless and tall,
Close the great doors, shut out the world, and shed
Your benediction on this drooping head.

MARTIN ARMSTRONG.

It was the Lovely Moon

It was the lovely moon—she lifted
Slowly her white brow among
Bronze cloud-waves that ebbed and drifted
Faintly, faintlier afar.
Calm she looked, yet pale with wonder,
Sweet in unwonted thoughtfulness,
Watching the earth that dwindled under
Faintly, faintlier afar.
It was the lovely moon that lovelike
Hovered over the wandering, tired
Earth, her bosom grey and dovelike
Hovering beautiful as a dove. . . .
The lovely moon: her soft light falling
Lightly on roof and poplar and pine—
Tree to tree whispering and calling,
Wonderful in the silvery shine
Of the round, lovely, thoughtful moon.

JOHN FREEMAN.

Stillness

When the words rustle no more,
    And the last work's done,
When the bolt lies deep in the door,
    And Fire, our Sun,
Falls on the dark-laned meadows of the floor:

When from the clock's last chime to the next chime
    Silence beats his drum,
And Space with gaunt grey eyes and her brother Time
    Wheeling and whispering come,
She with the mould of form and he with the loom of
    rhyme,

Then twittering out in the night my thought-birds flee,
    I am emptied of all my dreams:
    I only hear Earth turning, only see
    Ether's long bankless streams,
And only know I should drown if you
    Laid not your hand on me.

JAMES ELROY FLECKER.

Lights Out

I have come to the borders of sleep,
The unfathomable deep
Forest where all must lose
Their way, however straight,
Or winding, soon or late;
They cannot choose.

Many a road and track
That, since the dawn's first crack,
Up to the forest brink,

Deceived the travellers
Suddenly now blurs,
And in they sink.

Here love ends,
Despair, ambition ends,
All pleasure and all trouble,
Although most sweet or bitter,
Here ends in sleep that is sweeter
Than tasks most noble.

There is not any book
Or face of dearest look
That I would not turn from now
To go into the unknown
I must enter and leave alone
I know not how.

The tall forest towers,
Its cloudy foliage lowers
Ahead, shelf above shelf,
Its silence I hear and obey
That I may lose my way
And myself.

EDWARD THOMAS.

The Reaper

Behold her, single in the field,
Yon solitary Highland Lass!
Reaping and singing by herself;
Stop here, or gently pass!
Alone she cuts and binds the grain,
And sings a melancholy strain;
O listen! for the vale profound
Is overflowing with the sound.

No nightingale did ever chaunt
More welcome notes to weary bands
Of travellers in some shady haunt,
Among Arabian sands:
A voice so thrilling ne'er was heard
In springtime from the cuckoo-bird,
Breaking the silence of the seas
Among the farthest Hebrides.

Will no one tell me what she sings?
Perhaps the plaintive numbers flow
For old, unhappy, far-off things,
And battles long ago:
Or is it some more humble lay,
Familiar matter of to-day?
Some natural sorrow, loss or pain,
That has been, and may be again!

Whate'er the theme, the maiden sang
As if her song could have no ending;
I saw her singing at her work,
And o'er the sickle bending:
I listen'd, motionless and still,
And, as I mounted up the hill,
The music in my heart I bore
Long after it was heard no more.

WILLIAM WORDSWORTH.

From " The Princess "

Now sleeps the crimson petal, now the white;
Nor waves the cypress in the palace walk;
Nor winks the gold fin in the porphyry font;
The fire-fly wakens: waken thou with me.

232

Now droops the milkwhite peacock like a ghost,
And like a ghost she glimmers on to me.

Now lies the earth all Danäe to the stars,
And all thy heart lies open unto me.

Now slides the silent meteor on, and leaves
A shining furrow, as thy thoughts in me.

Now folds the lily all her sweetness up,
And slips into the bosom of the lake;
So fold thyself, my dearest, thou, and slip
Into my bosom and be lost in me.

TENNYSON.

Journey's End

What will they give me, when journey's done?
Your own room to be quiet in, Son!

Who shares it with me? There is none
shares that cool dormitory, Son!

Who turns the sheets? There is but one
and no one needs to turn it, Son.

Who lights the candle? Everyone
sleeps without candle all night, Son.

Who calls me after sleeping? Son,
You are not called when journey's done.

HUMBERT WOLFE.

Recovery

When this so bitter tide
Shall turn and ebb to the waste whence it came,
The world, like a wrecked ship shorn of her pride,
A battered ship, tipped on a riddled side,
A shattered ship, shall ride
From storm to port, bankrupt of all but shame.

In that dark dawn all we
As lost mariners shall reel crazily
On a new earth, grown stranger than the sea.
As drowned men shall we come,
All cold, all sick, all dumb.
(But some, some, some
Shall not thus come, so cold, so dumb they be.)

We'll have no words to string, no tales to tell
Of the unutterable
Black dreams dreamt in the drifting deeps of hell.
But common things of earth
Shall make us mirth.
Street lamps shall prick at cockshut down the street,
Brown ale foam up, fried fishes sizzle sweet;
Damp tap-room sawdust scrunch beneath our feet.

So, bankrupt of hope and blind
To faith and love, we'll find
Drugged laughter and peace in old things known and kind.
Though it lie drowned, the world we dreamt we knew,
Oh, though no dream be true,
We shall cry and laugh, as sailors and children do.

ROSE MACAULAY.

234

The White Island

In this world (the Isle of Dreams)
While we sit by sorrowes streames,
Tears and terrors are our theames
　　　Reciting :

But when once from hence we flie,
More and more approaching nigh
Unto young Eternitie
　　　Uniting :

In that whiter Island, where
Things are evermore sincere ;
Candor here, and lustre there,
　　　Delighting :

There no monstrous fancies shall
Out of hell an horrour call,
To create (or cause at all)
　　　Affrighting.

There in calm and cooling sleep
We our eyes shall never steep ;
But eternall watch shall keep
　　　Attending.

Pleasures, such as shall pursue
Me immortaliz'd, and you ;
And fresh joyes, as never to
　　　Have ending.

ROBERT HERRICK.

The Garden

Somewhere west there's a Garden
  Laid out with paths of peace,
That hath no other warden
Save, at the Gate of Pardon,
    The Angel of Release.

You'd never dream how deep is
  The hush of souls around,
Nor how untroubled sleep is,
Nor how the peace they keep is
    Fenced from human sound.

There's no noise of hearts breaking,
  Only, sometimes the sigh
Drifts in of tired souls shaking
Life's dust off softly and taking
    On immortality.

                    H. W. GARROD.

The Dawning

At what time wilt Thou come? When shall that cry
" The Bridegroom's coming ! " fill the sky?
Shall it in the evening run,
When our words and works are done?
Or will Thy all-surprising light
    Break at midnight,
  When either sleep, or some dark pleasure
Possesseth mad man without measure?
  Or shall these early, fragrant hours
    Unlock thy bowers?

And with their blush of light descry
Thy locks crowned with eternity?
Indeed, it is the only time
That with Thy glory doth best chime!
All now are stirring, every field
Full hymns doth yield;
The whole creation shakes off night,
And for Thy shadow looks, the light.
Stars now vanish without number,
Sleepy planets set and slumber,
The pursy clouds disband and scatter,
All expect some sudden matter!
Not one beam triumphs, but from far
    That morning-star.

O at what time soever Thou,
Unknown to us, the heavens wilt bow,
And with Thy angels in the van
Descend to judge poor careless man,
Grant I may not like puddle lie
In a corrupt security,
Where, if a traveller water crave,
He finds it dead, and in a grave;
But, as this restless, vocal spring
All day and night doth run and sing,
And, though here born, yet is acquainted
Elsewhere, and flowing keeps untainted;
So let me all my busy age
In Thy free services engage;
And though—while here—of force I must
Have commerce sometimes with poor dust,
And in my flesh, though vile and low,
(As this doth in her channel flow),
Yet let my course, my aim, my love,
And chief acquaintance be above.

So when that day and hour shall come,
In which Thy Self will be the sun,
Thou'lt find me dressed and on my way,
Watching the break of Thy great day.

HENRY VAUGHAN.

INDEX TO AUTHORS